D1738224

Presenting Miss Jane Austen

Also by May Lamberton Becker

Adventures in Reading
A Readers' Guide Book
Books as Windows
Under Twenty (editor)
Five Cats from Siam
Reading Menus for Young People: Chats about Much Loved Books Old and New
A Treasure Box of Stories for Children (editor)
First Adventures in Reading: Introducing Children to Books
"Golden Tales" series (editor), all illustrated by Lois Lenski
Introducing Charles Dickens (illustrated by Oscar Ogg)
The Home Book of Christmas (editor)
Youth Replies, I Can: Stories of Resistance (editor)
The Home Book of Laughter (editor)
"Rainbow Classics" series (editor)

Presenting
Miss Jane Austen

J. Austen

May Lamberton Becker

Illustrated by Edward Price

BETHLEHEM BOOKS · IGNATIUS PRESS
Bathgate   San Francisco

Originally published in 1952 by Dodd, Mead and Co.

Cover art © Lydia Halverson
Cover design by Theodore Schluenderfritz
Special features © 2006 Bethlehem Books

First Bethlehem Books Printing April, 2006

ISBN 978-1-932350-07-4
Library of Congress Catalog Number: 2005939019

Bethlehem Books • Ignatius Press
10194 Garfield Street South
Bathgate, North Dakota 58216
www.bethlehembooks.com
1-800-757-6831

Printed in the United States on acid-free paper

United Graphics Inc. Mattoon, IL, Second Printing May 2010

To

The Membership of

THE JANE AUSTEN SOCIETY

this work is
by its permission
most respectfully
dedicated

By the Society's

Dutiful
and obedient
HUMBLE SERVANT

THE AUTHOR

Acknowledgments

I have to acknowledge my indebtedness to Mr. R. A. Austen-Leigh, who at the outset of this book gave me the run of his library, showed me Jane Austen's Southampton, and permitted me to quote from *Austen Papers*.

To the Oxford University Press, for permission to quote from their publications.

To the Jane Austen Society, for its hospitality, especially on the day when the first reading from the manuscript of this book took place in the room where Jane Austen wrote, before a little group of its chosen spirits.

To Miss Dorothy Darnell, originator and Honorary Secretary of the Society at whose home, overlooking the landscape Jane loved, with sunset at the window, candle-light in the room and three around the fire, two chapters of this book were read—for her encouragement.

To Rev. Louis A. Brulant, Rector of North Waltham, who had the old registers brought out at Steventon Church that I might see Jane's entries, and the original Glebe map taken to Steventon that I might trace the site of the Old Rectory.

To Mr. Edward Price, Cheshunt, Herts, illustrator of

this book, for the care and enthusiasm with which he visited localities and searched sources.

To Miss Dorothy Bryan of Dodd, Mead and Company, for a long and happy association.

To the Reading Room of the British Museum for years of courteous hospitality extended to this reader, as to "readers only" the world over.

And to companionship through correspondence with the "elect company" of Janites who write to the *Herald Tribune's The Reader's Guide.*

Illustrations

Jane Austen: *A conjectural portrait by Edward C. Price,*
   derived from Cassandra's sketch
   and contemporary descriptions   *Frontispiece*

The Old Rectory at Steventon   4
   From a drawing by Anna Lefroy

A Riding Habit of the Period   6

Steventon Manor   8
   From a drawing by Anna Lefroy

George Austen Presenting Young Edward to
Mr. and Mrs. Thomas Knight   10
   "A charming group silhouette, cut
   to celebrate the event"

At the Abbey School   13

Mrs. George Austen   17
   From a silhouette

Rev. George Austen   21
   From a silhouette

Steventon Church   23

Eliza de Feuillide   30
    From a miniature

A Sofa   34

An Ornamental Bridge   45

Headdresses for a Ball   51

Tom Lefroy   54
    From a miniature
    "Thus in this light-hearted season
    Tom Lefroy was great fun"

Staircase for a Manor House   56

In a Phaeton   60

Cassandra Austen   65
    From a silhouette
    "Henceforth they would never be divided"

Mrs. Leigh Perrot   69
    ". . . her unbending portrait . . ."

Sidney Place, Bath   75

The Old Pump   77
    "Do not look for the Rectory when
    you go to Steventon"

Plan of Glebe Land at Steventon in 1821:   78
    showing the site of the Old Rectory

Manydown Park   83
    "... the great house where Jane used to break the
    journey to and from a Basingstoke Ball..."

The Crescent, Bath   87

Lyme Regis   90
    "The landscape of Lyme is so lovely that when Jane
    went home she took it with her"

The Cobb   91
    "That rugged old breakwater"

Chawton Cottage   99

Elizabeth and Darcy   108
    "When Darcy explodes into the
    world's prize proposal..."

The Topaz Crosses   116

"Worldly People"   122

"Most Precious Treasures"   136

Box Hill   140
    From a contemporary engraving

The Donkey Cart in Action   149
    "Jane's cart' which now has come
    back to Chawton Cottage..."

The House on College Street   152
    "There was nothing now to trouble her; to
    Winchester she could go in peace, without possessions"

"L'aimable Jane"   160
    Drawn from the silhouette so endorsed

"Letting in an Unknown and
Completely Charming Young Man"   174

PRESENTING MISS JANE AUSTEN

Chapter One

THE Rector of Steventon, his eyes shining, his tidy appearance a trifle upset—for it had been a busy day—opened his desk by the bay window overlooking the garden and prepared to write a letter that must not be delayed. Sister Susanna would be anxious; she had been waiting longer than anyone had expected. Now he wrote rapidly, in his clear, beautiful hand:

> … however, last night the time came, and without a great deal of warning, everything was soon happily over. We have now another girl, a present plaything for her sister Cassy and a future companion. She is to be Jenny, and seems to me as if she would be as like Henry, as Cassy is to Neddy. Your sister, thank God, is pure well after it, and sends her love to you and my brother, not forgetting James and Philly…

Adding that there would be a plowing match in the neighborhood on the following Tuesday, he left off with

> I am, dear sister,
> Your affecte. brother
> Geo. Austen.

folded the sheet to form its envelope, addressed it to Mrs. Walter at The Parsonage, near Tonbridge, Kent, and sent it off to the post-boy. Susanna would be sure to send it on. Family feeling was strong among the Austens. Though she was his half-brother's wife, he had addressed her as "Dear Sister"; no colder term would serve for one marrying into a family so warmhearted, where anything of importance to one was of interest to all; family connections were scattered over Southern England. This news would go rapidly round the circle. Standing at the window looking down the familiar path to the sundial—swept now by brisk winds on this winter day—he reflected comfortably how far the letter would go and how many would read what he had written.

Not being gifted with second sight, he could not foresee how far it would actually go in time and space, nor how many in centuries to come would read this note dated *Steventon, 17th December, 1775* with the interest generally reserved for their own personal mail.

Nor could he be aware that some of them in the twentieth century might be smiling as they read, to think how far from coming true one of his first predictions for the new daughter had been. He had written, "She is to be Jenny," and she never was. In the family at home she was Jane; Aunt Jane to the adoring nephews and nieces; Miss J. Austen beyond the circle of her intimate friends—till generations beyond her own began to know her as "dear, delightful Jane."

Chapter Two

THE rectory at Steventon, with its gardens and a big barn over at one side, stood at the end of a village street whose houses spread along either side. It was scarcely more than a large cottage in 1764 when George Austen married Miss Cassandra Leigh and settled here with his bride, but they straightway set out to remodel it for the large family they hoped to have and lost no time in accumulating.

All their children were good-looking. There was beauty on both sides of the family. At Oxford, George Austen had been known as "the handsome tutor" and even when he was seventy and had retired to Bath, he would be pointed out on the streets of that resort of fashion. Now, in the prime of life, with wife and family round him, his curly hair, prematurely white, bringing out the brightness of his eyes, he was not only good to look at but sweet-tempered—traits all the children inherited and kept all their lives.

Mrs. Austen's sister Jane was the beauty on her side; she herself cheerfully admitted that all she could bring to the Austen good looks was her aristocratic nose. Fortunately, the children inherited that, too, for Mrs. Austen had definite ideas about other people's noses and was "amusingly particular" regarding them. Indeed, all her ideas were definite,

not to say pronounced, but as they were also practical and often amusing, she carried them out without disturbance. For instance, in her wedding outfit was a handsome riding habit of a rich scarlet color. She must have been splendid on a horse, but early in her married life it was evident that she would not be on a horse for some time to come. So, as they needed the money for re-building and she would not have a new dress for the next two years, she looped up the skirt of the riding habit and wore it as a house-dress; warm and comfortable it was, too. Mrs. Austen had ideas like that, sensible, with a humorous twist. Etiquette was strict in her day, but it was still possible for the gentry to do, within reason, pretty much as they pleased, and the Rector's family on both sides had long been gentry. The Austens had taken high places in the learned professions; the "loyal Leighs" went back to the Norman Conquest, taking in along the way the Lord Mayor of London behind whom Queen Elizabeth walked in procession to Paul's Cross. When ladies paid calls on young Mrs. Austen, born a Leigh, she not only received them in this glowing costume, but instead of keeping her hands folded in her lap, kept a mending-basket in the parlor and as they talked, operated on the family stockings. This was not customary conduct, but Mrs. Austen was nice about it; if the visitors did not like to see her do the mending, they were at liberty to stay away. It speaks well for her as a hostess that no one did.

The scarlet habit lasted till the little boys began to scamper across country on anything they could find to ride; then she cut it up into little coats and trousers. Fortunately, in the year she was married, fashion called for habits to have particularly full and flowing skirts; there was enough in hers to go a long way, and the scarlet petticoat must have lit up the landscape considerably.

For by the time Jane was born, the year before the Declaration of Independence, there was a houseful of boys. James, the oldest, was ten and her only sister, Cassandra, three when she arrived. None of the boys went away to school; their father loved to teach and could make boys love to learn and as long as his sons were of school age there were a few pupils living in the family, who studied with them. James the scholarly, Henry the brilliant, were prepared by their father for Oxford, where each of them distinguished himself in his own way.

All the children—save "poor little George," the second son who never came home from the cottage where he was put out to nurse—had robust, open-air constitutions. The big, square-fronted house with its line of dormer windows piercing the roof and its pair of wings at the back, now had three sitting rooms, seven bedrooms and two attics, and by

the time all the children were born might have been a tight fit for a family less even-tempered. But the Steventon Austens, happy by nature and disciplined by training to let others be happy, would have scorned a family quarrel and family differences were laughed over rather than dwelt upon.

James, the studious, had taken his degree at the University before Jane had ended her brief career at boarding school, and was glad to take an interest, second only to her father's, in directing her education. Tall, slender, dark-eyed, with a sensitive, thoughtful expression, he loved to have this engaging little sister come to him with what she had read. It was so entertaining to talk it over with her.

You must be prepared for surprises in the story of the Austens; all at once the quiet scene will be lit up by a sudden flash of the unexpected and something very like a fairy tale take place in real life. So it was with Edward, the third son. Starting life with the family good looks, a friendly disposition and a winning smile, it was soon clear that he would never be a devoted student of Latin. He never had to be. He was soon translated. Thomas Knight of Godmersham Park in Kent and Chawton Manor in Hampshire, whose father had appointed George Austen to Steventon, also owned most of that parish but he did not live there. The Rector of Steventon, his representative, thus had the social standing of a landed proprietor; the two families kept in touch. The Knights, a devoted couple, had no children. They thought about the Rector's boys, and as James was to follow his father in the church, decided that a letter should be sent inviting little Edward to make them a visit in the holidays. His father was rather against his going; the boy's Latin grammar might be neglected—and considering what little Edward thought of it, it probably would be. But his mother said, "I think,

my dear, you had better oblige your cousin and let the child
go." He went, and so won the hearts of the Knights that
when the holidays were over and Edward had returned to
Steventon, they knew they could not be happy till he came
back. So they adopted him and made him their heir, and as
a country gentleman with large estates and fortune would
not need so much Latin grammar, he was not prepared for
the University but to take the Grand Tour of Europe when
he should be old enough.

A charming group silhouette, cut to celebrate this event,
shows George Austen presenting young Edward to his new
family; the father's hands are on the shoulders of the little
fellow as with outstretched arms Edward sets out to run to
Mrs. Knight, who turns from the chess table while her husband beams from behind her chair. Everybody looks pleased
as possible, and so they continued to be. Edward became

the son of the Knights' dreams, but his affection for his first family never faded and he never lost touch with them. Being the sort of person whose idea of happiness is to make others happy, he found occasions to make them so.

Henry was the handsomest and the most versatile of the Austen boys; one of his charms was that whatever he was doing, he would soon be doing something else. He kept this up long after boyhood; it might have caused serious head shaking in a family all of whose other members chose one career and stuck to it, had not his impulses been so interesting. Whatever he did or said, he could not help being amusing. He learned so quickly that his father expected great things of him at the University; he took his degree and went into the Oxfordshire Militia. His square cap and academic gown had turned the heads of young ladies, but the scarlet uniform was even more attractive—even to himself—until he shot off at another angle and became something else. At home in Steventon his little sister found him delightful. A large family, however united, is bound to pair off within its limits; Henry and Jane were all their lives such a pair, less because they were so much alike as because from the first their differences fitted so well together. Jane could always say, "What a Henry!"

After Henry came the first daughter, Cassandra, just enough ahead of Jane on the Steventon roster to grow up with "a present plaything and a future companion" in her adoring little sister. But another son, Francis, had come before Jane did, and after her another, Charles, so these four were together at home until the two "sailor brothers" went off, each at twelve years old, to the Naval Academy to begin the careers that would in time make them both admirals.

Long before that, Francis had shown a certain talent for

getting things done without undue friction. Loving as he did to be in the midst of things, he had at an early age found a way of getting into a room he had not been invited to enter. Countryfolk visiting the servants and meaning to stay but a short time would say that they "were not come to bide." Francis, with the Austen interest in words, pounced on the phrase. When he heard voices behind a closed door and was not sure of his welcome, those on the inside would see the door gently open, ever so little, and a mop of curls appear through the crack, and would hear a little voice say, "Me no come to bide!" If no one objected—and what Austen would under the circumstances?—Francis would follow his curls into the company.

When he was seven he brought off the one brilliant financial transaction of his career—indeed the only one on the record of the Rectory. On his own account he bought a pony for a pound, named it Squirrel (his brothers insisted on calling it Scug), hunted it for two years, being especially keen on the jumps, and at the end of that time sold it for two pounds twelve and six.

Charles, always to be to the sisters "our own particular little brother," closed the ranks of the family. Like Francis, he was in later years to brave danger and win distinction on the other side of the world, and so win hearts that his death on the Irawaddy River—at seventy-three—was "a great grief to the whole fleet." Now, not in the least spoilt by being the family pet, he was a laughing, lighthearted little boy.

But who, among all these brothers, is this little, round-cheeked, rosy sister, too shy to leave the shelter of Cassandra's skirt when company calls, but looking out from it with bright-eyed interest?

That is Jane.

Chapter Three

SIX-YEAR-OLD Jane went away to school because Cassandra was going and, as her mother forcefully expressed it, "if Cassandra were ordered to have her head cut off, Jane would insist on sharing her fate." So the little lamb followed Cassy to a little school at Oxford kept by a widowed relative-in-law who was prepared to take a few little girls into her home as pupils. Her preparation for teaching seems to have been not more than that her husband had been principal of one of the Oxford colleges, but cousin Jane Cooper was going, so Cassandra went. So did Jane, who promptly fell ill and nearly lost her life.

For Mrs. Cawley, the relative-in-law, moved to Southampton, taking along the little girls, and there the young Austens caught what was then called a "putrid fever"—probably diphtheria—and Mrs. Cawley, thinking she could cope with it, did not notify their mother at home. Finally little Jane Cooper, frightened half out of her wits at Jane's condition, managed to get word to her own mother and Mrs. Austen. They came at top speed, Mrs. Austen found Jane almost at the point of death, nursed her back from it and brought her home to recover. But lovely Mrs. Cooper,

who also caught the fever, did not recover. However, this did not discourage Jane's parents from another attempt. This time the Austen girls were sent to the Abbey School at Reading.

If the Rector had, as I suspect, sent his little girls away to school lest so many boys at home should overwhelm their manners, the Abbey was surely a place where they could cultivate the graces. It was kept by Mrs. Latournelle, an old lady, active in spite of a cork leg. How she had lost that leg was one of the school mysteries; she never spoke of it, preferring to talk, outside of school matters, chiefly about the stage and the lives of theatrical people. For all her French name, she could not speak a word of French;

her specialty was giving out the laundry, planning meals, and other housekeeping matters, but she knew what good teachers should be and chose them wisely. Such boarders as wanted an education could get one. When one of the young lady boarders lost her money, Mrs. Latournelle took her on as partner, and much of the school's later success was due to her and to the French master she married. The latter's social connections in troubled France made the Abbey a center for noble exiles crossing the Channel.

The sisters from Steventon, used as they were at home to pleasant surroundings, could scarcely have made their first contact with the world in a pleasanter place. The school was built around the gateway of an abbey founded in 1125; this had rooms above, and on either side a vast staircase whose balustrades had once been gilt. You could look off a long way from its top, over the surrounding country; the rest of the buildings were enclosed by the wall of a large and thoroughly romantic garden. Of this the school's pupils, little girls and young ladies, were free; indeed, the young ladies, once they had attended a single class and put in an appearance at morning prayers, could do much as they pleased, with no one to ask, "Where have you been?" Little round-eyed Jane, keeping well within shelter of Cassandra among the flowers, could watch the older girls passing from sunlight to shadow under the tall trees, their lightly floating muslins appearing and reappearing, their young voices rising and falling as little groups formed and dissolved. It might not have been so satisfactory an occupation for an active eight-year-old as rolling down the grassy bank at the back of the Rectory—Jane's favorite outdoor sport at this time of life—but it was not so hard on clothes.

In time the school moved on, to London and later to

Napoleon's Paris, gathering prestige as it went. Some of its pupils, grown famous themselves, wrote recollections of their schooldays. One of them, Mrs. Sherwood, author of *The Fairchild Family*, born the same year as Jane but going to Reading when she was older, remembered and wrote of the garden as one recalls the happiness of a dream.

It was only as a dream that anything about the Abbey School stayed with Jane. She was not yet nine years old when she came home with Cassandra and never went back. Her formal education was over; her real schooling was now to begin.

Chapter Four

THE garden at the Rectory was not so large or so romantic as the one at the Abbey School, but it was a great deal more fun. Its friendly flowers came back punctually every year—syringas in sweet, snowy clusters, clumps of rosy peonies, heartsease white and purple, gold tassels on the laburnum near the house. There were rows of flowers planted among the rows of vegetables, strawberries bordered the walk to the sundial, and under the neighboring hedgerows—in this part of the country, as you sometimes still may find, hedgerows were double—the first wild primroses and violets bloomed before the spring. Besides, at the back was the grassy, sloping bank down which young Jane at once renewed acquaintance with one rapid roll.

A little lady could not have done that if a governess had been looking after her, but at the Rectory there was no governess—to everybody's satisfaction. Families of social standing usually had one in the house for their daughters. Seven years such little girls would spend in the nursery; then they would cross the hall to the schoolroom where a resident governess would for the next ten years take charge. Fifty pounds a year would be a good salary for this young

person. For that she would be expected to start the girls on some instrument—the pianoforte, or the harp, now becoming so fashionable—show them how to read music and copy it into their manuscript books, and perhaps to sing as many as three songs, usually in Italian, and to speak some French. Masters would come to take them further along any of these paths should they show talent. It was taken for granted that they would be set copies to form a clear, graceful hand, and would make a ladylike contact with arithmetic, and that their spelling—though this was not so important—should be looked after. General information reached these girls chiefly through books like *Mangnall's Questions*, small enough to slip into a pinafore pocket, whose answers, memorized just as they stood, were expected to slip into their heads and stay there. The two Miss Bertrams, the young ladies of *Mansfield Park*, might not have known as much as they thought they did when they marveled at the ignorance of their ten-year-old cousin from Portsmouth, "playfellow, instructress and nurse" of her own little brothers and sisters, who had never learned French:

"Dear Mamma, only think, my cousin cannot put the map of Europe together—or my cousin cannot tell the principal rivers in Russia—or she never heard of Asia Minor—or she does not know the difference between water-colors and crayons! How strange! …I am sure I should have been ashamed of myself, if I had not known better long before I was so old as she is. I cannot remember the time when I did not know a great deal that she has not the least notion of yet. How long ago it is … since we used to repeat the chronological order of the kings of England, with the dates of their accession, and most of the principal events of their reigns!"

"Yes," added the other; "and of the Roman emperors as low as Severus; besides a great deal of the Heathen mythology, and all the Metals, Semi-Metals, Planets and distinguished philosophers."

When their aunt—when you come to meet Mrs. Norris in *Mansfield Park* you will see that this would be just like her!—reminded them that they were "blessed with wonderful memories, and your poor cousin has probably none at all," Mrs. Norris went on

... And remember that, if you are ever so forward and clever yourselves, you should always be modest; for, much as you know already, there is a great deal more for you to learn."

"Yes, I know there is, till I am seventeen."

Then, of course, the Bertram young ladies would "come out" into society, shut the schoolroom door with the question-book inside, and never think of it again.

Not so young Jane. She might not have committed so much to memory, but she remembered what she read, and could scarcely recall a time when she could not read. In her father's personal library at Steventon were far more books than one would find in a country house of its size today, now that public libraries are so accessible.

What one loves, one remembers; to be guided through these chosen, treasured books was to learn to love the best in English literature. We have Henry Austen's word for it that at the Rectory no one ever heard a word of slang or bad grammar. No one had to struggle against either; they simply were not there and never had been there. It was the perfect atmosphere for one who was to write pure English that would also be completely natural English.

Through poetry new and old Jane's father guided her reading; better still, he read aloud to the family—history, travel books, lively essays in the *Rambler* and the *Spectator* —when James was at Oxford he edited his own periodical of this sort, the *Loiterer*, to which both he and Henry contributed. The whole family read *The Vicar of Wakefield, Sir Charles Grandison* and the novels of Miss Fanny Burney whose people were spoken of in the family as if they lived just round the corner—as Miss Jane Austen's people are spoken of now.

Jane was remembering all this when she wrote of one of her heroines who had others to teach her French or hear her read her daily portion of history, "but it was he who recommended the books which charmed her leisure hours, he made reading useful by talking to her of what she read and heightened its attractions by judicious praise." *

Don't take too seriously Miss Austen's later statement, when she was at the height of her powers, that "I think I may boast myself to be, with all possible vanity, the most unlearned and uninformed female who ever dared to be an authoress." Bear in mind that she wrote this, as you will see, in reply to the librarian of the Prince Regent, a somewhat pompous clergyman who wanted her to "delineate in some future novel the habits of life and character of a clergyman who should pass his time between the metropolis and the country," with some observations on the subject of tithes. She meant, without hurting his feelings, to let him know

* *Mansfield Park.*

that she was not going to do it. She never had a classical education, but no one ever had a more useful one. What she learned, like what she saw and heard, became part of her life; what she was to write has become part of ours.

But that was far ahead. No one as yet had expected such a thing as that the Prince Regent himself would ask Jane to dedicate a novel to him—one of the few things he did that was so sensible one wonders why he did it. Ladies of quality living in the country did not write novels and get them published—except of course Miss Fanny Burney, but she lived in London among actors like the great Garrick and musicians like her father Dr. Burney, and had actually known Doctor Johnson whom nobody could be like. Ladies in the country contented themselves with writing letters—especially the Austens, who believed that "cousins should *be* cousins and take an interest in each other." Correspondence held their wide circle together, and whatever else there might be in Jane's lessons, she had to learn to write a clear, easy-running and—because postage was expensive—a small hand. And that took practice.

Hers was so neat and tidy the Rector sometimes brought home the parish register, kept in the church beyond the garden walk, and let her make the entries of births, deaths and marriages. This is why we have an early example of her handwriting that will endear her to many a small girl. Before a wedding could take place in church the clergyman must "publish the banns of matrimony" by reading to the congregation, three times in succession on a Sunday, that So-and-So meant to marry So-and-So, and entry must be made in the parish register to this effect. To show just how entries should be made, one page of the big book had printed forms with the names of the contracting parties blank. Now

Jane had the run of the register, and though she would not for the world have tampered with the record, I have yet to find an intelligent ten-year-old who could resist filling in blanks in a matrimonial form that is not going to be used. So if you make your way along the wood path to the little church today and the verger, on request, opens the chest where the records are kept, you will see that on a date unspecified the Banns of Marriage were published between Henry Frederic Howard Fitzwilliam of London and Jane Austen of Steventon, and just below, that Edmund Arthur William Mortimer of London and Jane Austen of Steventon were married, on a date also unspecified. Jane had at that time spacious ideas on names. However, the short form hadn't room enough for more than that "Marriage was solemnized between us, Jack Smith, Jane Smith late Austen."

So the big book goes back into the chest in the little room back of the Squire's pew, and everyone who sees it comes away with a curious sense of having met young Jane in person—and wondering what the Rector did when he found this information on the books. No record remains, but from everything in his character I am sure he tried to swallow a smile and advised her not to do it again. He knew she would not. There were no more forms of the sort left to be filled.

Jane's handwriting did appear, however, in her copy of Oliver Goldsmith's *History of England, in a Series of Letters from a Nobleman to his Son,* written for young people but rapidly adopted for household equipment. In a marginal note addressing the author as "My dear Mr. G.," she told him firmly that she agreed with him on one of his statements. Young Jane took a lively view of history. When she was fifteen she wrote a history of her own for family consumption only, and Cassandra illustrated it with portraits in watercolor. When it was read aloud, the fireside audience began to chuckle before the end of the title:

> *A History of England, from the Reign of Henry the 4th to the death of Charles the 1st, by a partial, prejudiced and ignorant historian. N.B. There will be very few dates in this history.*

In regard to Henry VI Jane cheerfully submits that

> I cannot say much for this Monarch's sense. Nor would I if I could, for he was a Lancastrian. I suppose you know all about the Wars between him and the Duke of York, who was of the right side; if you do not, you had better read some other History, for I shall not be very diffuse in this, meaning by it only to vent my

spleen *against* and show my Hatred *to* all those people whose parties or principles do not suit with mine, and not to give information.

The family, familiar as they were with popular histories of the period which took sides so sharply, appreciated that bit! So they did the outburst on behalf of Mary, Queen of Scots; the "loyal Leighs" had stood by Bonnie Prince Charlie:

O what must have this bewitching Princess whose only friend was then the Duke of Norfolk, and whose only ones now Mr. Whitaker, Mrs. Lefroy, Mrs. Knight and myself, who was abandoned by her son, confined by her Cousin, abused, reproached and vilified by all, what must not her noble mind have suffered when informed that Elizabeth had given orders for her death?

Indeed the bewitching Princess quite runs away with the story until the young historian pulls up with:

It may not be unnecessary before I entirely conclude my account of this ill-fated Queen, to observe that she had been accused of several crimes during the time of her reigning in Scotland, of which I now most seriously do assure my Readers that she was entirely innocent; having never been guilty of anything more than Imprudencies into which she was betrayed by the openness of her Heart, her Youth and her Education. Having I trust by this assurance entirely done away every Suspicion and every doubt which might have arisen in the Reader's mind, from what other Historians have written of her, I shall proceed to mention the remaining events that marked Elizabeth's reign.

Henry VIII is neatly disposed of:

> It would be an affront to my Readers were I to sup-
> pose that they were not as well acquainted with the
> particulars of this King's reign as I am myself. It will
> therefore be saving *them* the task of reading again what
> they have read before, and *myself* the trouble of writing
> what I do not perfectly recollect, by giving only a slight
> sketch of the principal Events that marked his reign.

This was not the sort of treatment history was getting
then from historians. It is far more like that it lately received
from two very modern historians, Messrs. Sellar and Yeat-
man, in that priceless spoof, *1066 and All That*.

Chapter Five

YOUNG Jane was already finding people, past or present, uncommonly entertaining. Under her candid gaze some of them were a trifle uneasy. Could it be, they thought for a bleak moment, that she was actually finding *them* funny ? But as such people would never believe that possible, they promptly dismissed the idea, thought of the Rector's younger daughter—if at all—as "prim" or "whimsical," and went on criticizing others instead of enjoying them as they were.

Jane, though as yet she scarcely knew it, was taking notes. The village, the visitors, the cousins, already gave her plenty to store away, back of those bright eyes. And now, before her teens set in, someone was coming who would bring with her the great world.

This was the Comtesse de Feuillide, who began life as Betsy Hancock and ended it as Eliza Austen.

Her mother was George Austen's sister Philadelphia, who had been sent out to India on a visit with the underlying idea that among all those rich English residents would be a prospective husband. She married Tysoe Hancock, much older than herself and not so very rich, but the great Warren Hastings, his friend, stood godfather to their only child, gave her the name he had chosen for his daughter who did not live to bear it, and established a trust fund for this little Eliza. When she was four the Hancocks brought her to England, meaning themselves to stay. However, living at the scale to which they had been used in India cost so much more in England that her father—now tired, ill, and hoping only "that I may live long enough to provide for you and my dear Betsy"—went back to India and died there.

But Betsy's education went on as the letters of the lonely old man had directed. She had the little horse to ride gracefully and without fear, the harpsichord on which to be taught "the Fundamentals of Musick, and if she attempts the Guitar let her be careful not to pick up a wrong method of fingering. As soon as possible she must begin to learn Arithmetick; her other accomplishments will be ornaments to her, but these are most absolutely necessary." If a French governess should be absolutely necessary too, for the sake of a good accent, the governess must not stay "till the Child may be old enough to imbibe the Spirit of Intrigue without which no French Woman ever yet existed."

Whatever else Eliza imbibed along with the French language, she spoke it perfectly before her seventeenth year, and though the Rector, whom she loved best among her guardians, had not thought much of her mother's taking her to France to finish her education, there she had been, enjoying herself vastly in the highest social circles of Paris.

Her delight overflowed in letters to the English cousins, and Philadelphia Walter, Susanna's daughter, passed hers round. All the cousins learned through these round robins how much powder was used in hairdressing, so that "heads in general look as if they had been dipped in a meal tub," and that the fashionable hats called English "do not bear the least resemblance to those of our nation"—which one can well believe. "No wonder," wrote the enchanted girl as so many others have written to relatives at home, "there is perhaps no place in the world where dress is so well understood & carried to so great a perfection as in Paris, & no wonder it should be so, since people make it the chief business & study of their lives."

The daughters of the Rectory did not go so far as that. They were wearing the simple frocks of little girls. But they were born with good taste and at an early age thought about pretty clothes as much as two girls might be expected to do if they were on the way to be spoken of as "perfect beauties." They still wore pinafores, but they could think about muslins sprigged or spotted, about "pink Persian," about delicate colors, though of course white was best—a lady could never be "too fine" whose dress was white, especially if it were soft, filmy and with glossy spots. They knew that they would have more thought than money to spend on clothes when they were old enough to go to dances; they were resolved—and always kept that resolution—never to run into debt for anything. Under these conditions a charming dress would be a triumph in itself, but they meant to manage it gracefully when their time came—and they did. Still, it was fascinating now to hear about Eliza's clothes, managed just as gracefully and less economically.

Presently came something even more fascinating—the painted miniature of a lovely laughing little lady, looking with complete self-possession out of the French court. Here was Eliza to the life, tiptoe on top of the world, expecting affection and offering it to the uncle she loved and the cousins she was ready to love. Eliza was on the horizon of Steventon like a permanent rainbow and likely to stay there,

however she might talk of coming home.

For handsome young Jean Capotte, Comte de Feuillide, with great connections and expectations, was in love with her and though her family in England wrote back and forth to each other that Uncle George Austen was "much concerned at the connection which he says is giving up all their friends, their country, and he fears, their religion," there was no doubt that Eliza was very ready to have Jean.

Their wedding came in a brilliant year. The birth of the Dauphin was making Paris particularly gay, with Marie

Antoinette at the height of her beauty. The birthday ball under eight thousand lights—so soon and so tragically to be blacked out—came to England in Eliza's letter like a scene from the Arabian Nights:

> … Her Majesty, who is handsome at all times, had her charms not a little heightened by the magnificence of her adjustment. It was a kind of Turkish dress made of a silver-grounded silk intermixed with blue & entirely trimmed & almost covered with jewels. A sash and tassels of diamonds went round her waist, her sleeves were puffed & confined in several places with diamonds, large knots of the same fastened a flowing veil of silver gauze; her hair which is remarkably handsome was adorned with the most beautiful jewels of all kinds intermixed with flowers & a large plume of white feathers …*

That was in 1782, while Jane was still at the Abbey. There were rumblings and shakings in France. Four years later, when Her Majesty was shivering at the very thought of diamond necklaces, there was good reason for Comte de Feuillide to wish his son to be born in England. Just before the event Eliza came over with her mother and after it enjoyed the racketing of a London life with the same light heart. It had been a warm heart for the Rectory ever since, as a tiny girl, she had fallen in love with her dear Uncle George, who got on so well with all children but had a special fondness for bright ones. Now the Duchess of Cumberland's ball, presentation at court and going to all the new plays in

---

* Quoted by permission from Austen Papers 1704-1856 edited by R. A. Austen-Leigh. Privately printed.

London were delightful to her, but so was the prospect of meeting once more the members of the Rectory family who had been growing up while she was out of England— Cassandra, for instance, and that little Jane who must by this time be near her teens.

Besides, there would be theatricals this Christmas in the Rectory at Steventon.

Chapter Six

THEATRICALS at the Rectory had to be held in the holidays. Large as the house was, there would not be room enough in it till the pupils went home. Indeed, Mrs. Austen let it be known that there would not be room enough, even then, for any lazy young people. If they came, they must Act.

The performances had begun simply enough, developing from homemade charades; all the Austens were good at writing charades and acting them out. Then they began to give plays in the parlor, with a single line of chairs against the wall for the audience and scenery that had to be helped out by the audience's imagination. But no one could stop there with a big barn just across the road and a village carpenter who could be shown how to run up a side-wing or two with doors in flat and three or four scenes to let down.

Choosing a play strewed the house with little pamphlets, acting editions of London stage successes. Everybody read them all, Jane included. For the first production in the barn they chose one that had been a great success the year Jane was born, when Sheridan put it on—*The Rivals*. The young people pleased themselves so much in it that this time they

were to give two; Mrs. Cowley's *Which is the Man?* and David Garrick's *Bon Ton.* The wonderful cousin from Paris had seen them acted at Tonbridge Wells. In each was a part in which she felt she could do herself justice, so their leading lady was assured.

So was her welcome by the family, into whose life she instantly fitted to a charm. Jane, the curly-haired twelve-year-old, still too shy to put her admiration into words, could not conceal it. Eliza was delighted with both girls at first sight. Cassandra was more grown-up and, she admitted, more beautiful—it was fortunate for her that she did admit it; Jane would never have forgiven her had she not. But how could Eliza's heart resist loving Jane just a little better, especially since she could not help seeing how much Jane admired her? Jane's clear eyes saw that Eliza was not perfect, but Eliza herself knew that perfectly well. It was wonderful to her that so young a creature could see her, not perhaps as she was, but just as she saw herself in the glass! One who could do that, would be dear to her all her life.

Both plays went off beautifully. In *Which is the Man?*, Henry, as the lead, spoke the epilogue in the regimentals of the British Soldier it praised. The little countess in the large hoop in which she had danced at Almack's till five in the morning, made sure that *Lady Bell Bloomer* lived up to her reputation as the model of an English gentlewoman. But *Bon Ton* might have been written for her, not as the heroine but as *Miss Tittup*, the girl who flirts up to the edge of danger but escapes because "I find that my English heart, though it ventures so far, grows too fearful and awkward to practice the freedom of warmer climates." Born in India, brought up in France, Eliza de Feuillide had an English heart.

Next Christmas she was thinking with affection of the gaiety that would be going on in the barn. They were giving Garrick's *The Sultan* this year. Henry, taller than ever, would be magnificent as the *Sultan*, but a comparatively insipid cousin had to be called on to play the spirited *Roxalana*, the English slave there was no bearing because "she says such things and she does such things!" Eliza could see in her looking glass just the face for *Roxalana*, of whom it was said, "Who would have thought that a little cock'd up nose would have overturned the customs of a mighty empire?" Life was trembling with excitement where she was—but she read the lines with a little longing.

Jane was not one of the actors, but there was not a part

she could not have taken. Sometimes prompter, sometimes hearing the players say their lines, sometimes as encouraging spectator, she was in the midst of everything, seeing more than the cast. Indeed, she was seeing through a great deal that an audience was supposed to accept. Fathers, for instance, in some of these acting editions had to do a vast deal of explaining before the action could start. Sometimes they must open the first scene by telling somebody, who knew it already, what it was all about. Jane beat them at this. In her *First Act of a Comedy*, offered to the family circle and going no further, she got it all into one sentence:

Enter POPGUN and PISTOLETTA
PISTOLETTA: Pray, papa, how far is it to London?
POPGUN: My Girl, my Darling, my favorite of all
my children, who art the picture of thy
poor mother, who died two months ago,
with whom I am going to town to marry
to Strephon and to whom I mean to Be-
queath my whole Estate, it wants seven
miles.

The "aside" was in full bloom just then. Young Jane glee-fully used it to the full in

THE MYSTERY
an Unfinished Comedy
DEDICATION
to the Rev'd George Austen

Sir: I humbly solicit your Patronage to the following Comedy, which tho' an unfinished one, I flatter myself as *complete a mystery* as any of its kind.

I am, sir, your most Humble Servant,

The Author.

ACT THE FIRST

Scene the First

A Garden

Enter CORYDON

CORY.: But Hush! I am interrupted. (Exit CORY-
DON) (Enter OLD HUMBUG and his
son, talking)

OLD HUM.: It is for that reason I wish you to follow
my advice. Are you convinced of its
propriety ?

YOUNG HUM.: I am, sir, and will certainly act in
the manner you have pointed out
to me.

OLD HUM.: Then let us return to the House. (Exeunt)

Scene the 2ⁿᵈ

A Parlor in the Humbugs' House

MRS. HUMBUG and FANNY, *discovered at work*

MRS. HUM.: You understand me, my love?

FANNY: Perfectly, madam. Pray continue your nar-
rative.

MRS. HUM.: Alas! it is nearly concluded, for I have
nothing more to say on the subject.

FANNY: Ah! here's DAPHNE.

DAPHNE: My dear Mrs. Humbug how d'ye do? Oh!
Fanny 'tis all over.

FANNY: Is it indeed!

MRS. HUM.: I'm very sorry to hear it.

FANNY: Then 'twas to no purpose that I ...

DAPHNE: None upon Earth.

MRS. HUM.: And what's to become of ... ?

DAPHNE: Oh! that's all settled. (Whispers MRS. HUMBUG).

FANNY: And how is it determined ?

DAPHNE: I'll tell you. (Whispers FANNY).

MRS. HUM.: And is he to ... ?

DAPHNE: I'll tell you all I know of the matter. (Whispers MRS. HUMBUG and FANNY).

FANNY: Well! now I know everything about it, I'll go away.

MRS. HUM.:
DAPHNE: And so will I.

(Exeunt)

Scene the 3d

The Curtain rises and discovers Sir Edward Spangle
reclined in an elegant Attitude on a Sofa, fast asleep.

Enter COLONEL ELLIOTT

COLONEL: My Daughter is not here I see ... there
lies Sir Edward ... Shall I tell him the
secret? ... No, he'll certainly blab it ...
But he's asleep and won't hear me ... So
I'll e'en venture.

(Goes up to Sir Edward, whispers him and
EXIT)

End of the 1st Act

FINIS

When the family round the fire in the evening were

laughing over this, Eliza was not in the audience.

Soon there would be no more theatricals in the barn.

The Reign of Terror had begun in France. Word came to the Comte de Feuillide, in England with his wife and child, that if he did not instantly return, he would be denounced as an émigré and all his property confiscated. He went back and was guillotined.

The French Revolution was no longer across the Channel. It had struck straight at the heart of the quiet Rectory.

Chapter Seven

IN Steventon, life closed over the calamity. The ground was still firm under their little world, however the great world outside might be shaking. History was coming in across the Channel by every courier—a strange new history in the making, so far from what they meant by the word that to them this "Rebellion in France" was less the end of a world, still less the beginning of a new one, than a tragic break in the order of things. There had been such breaks before: this one would close over. The fire in France would burn out. Fires always did, in time.

So time went quietly among the Austens, who had all read history books. There were other books to read aloud.

Some people like to read aloud, some to listen to reading; the same person rarely likes to do both, but all the Austens did, and they took turns. When curtains were drawn, candles lit and the sisters were embroidering under this gentle flame or stitching at those interminable handmade shirts with which young ladies were expected to equip their brothers, the Rector, as he opened a book, knew the family would enjoy it as much as he did. It might be poetry— Crabbe, or Cowper, or Scott. It might be a novel like *Sir Charles*

Grandison. It might be a thriller of the period, such as the Minerva Press in Leadenhall Street, London, could hardly turn out fast enough to meet the demand. Horace Walpole had set off the fashion—the furore you might call it—for Gothic romances, with his *Castle of Otranto*; Mrs. Radcliffe's *Mysteries of Udolpho* brought it to a climax—that grand gloomy amazing romance that shortened the hours of sleep for so many young ladies and, according to their own admissions, for not a few elderly gentlemen. There certainly was something about *Mysteries of Udolpho* and indeed there still is; whoever starts it has to go on with his eyes glued to the page at least till he finds out What is Behind the Black Veil! The people in the book have marched in at one eye and out at the other, leaving no trace, but around 1790, when those wild majestic scenes began to roll, every patron of a lending library was caught and carried along by a current of suspense until he was cast up on the last page, panting for more. Mrs. Radcliffe gave them more, and so did her followers and imitators. It was a style of romance that nobody believed and everybody read, most of them because it made them shudder and some of them because it made them laugh.

The Austens enjoyed these "horrid" novels much as we now enjoy an occasional shocker; they could take them or leave them. They had more fun with the long-winded sentimental romances that came in when the demand for horrors began to fall off. These heroines were persecuted, too, but they did not have to stand it for so long at a time. They could always faint, and they did, all over the place. Their sensibility was so great a sigh could blow them over. In real life a healthy girl could not faint as easily as all that —but how often she wished she could! Every young woman knows that social situations may arise that can be met only by a good swift faint. These heroines of fiction were equipped to meet them. When Thomas Babington Macaulay had grown up and was in India, one of these romances dear to his youth was put up for auction there and he jumped at the chance to recover a copy at any cost. So did Miss Emily Eden. They bid against each other in memory of past joys till Macaulay won the book at a huge price: the auctioneer couldn't imagine why. The book was Mrs. Kitty Cuthbertson's *Santo Sebastiano*, or *The Young Pretender*, and on the last page of Macaulay's copy, in his handwriting, is a list that shows why he bid for it, bought it, and with what affectionate care treasured it. For it records the number of fainting fits that occur in the course of its four (small) volumes:

Julia de Clifford	11
Lady Delamore	4
Lady Theodosia	4
Lord Glenbrook	2
Lady Enderfield	1
Lord Ashgrove	1
Lord St. Orville	1
Henry Mildmay	1.

To this total Lord St. Orville, it will be seen, contributed but one faint, but this was a beauty: "One of the sweetest smiles that ever animated the face of mortal now diffused itself over the face of Lord St. Orville, as he fell at the feet of Julia in a deathlike swoon." With a record of eleven swoons of her own, Julia was no doubt able to bring him to.

Chapter Eight

NOT for a moment did one of those fainting ladies take in young Jane, much as they amused her. People like that—only funnier—could be made out of no more than ink and white paper. It would be harder, she knew very well, to put real human beings on paper just as they were—a glimpse here, a speech there. It would not be easy, but it could be done. She had already tried her hand at it. In the little dressing room beyond the square chamber over the front door where the sisters slept, were bits and pieces saved to show Cassandra, who thought them wonderful—more wonderful than Jane did. Enough of these bits and pieces had been gathered to fill three copybooks. Part of one held something complete, a burlesque running light as laughter, a little novel in letters after the fashion of the day. It was called *Love and Freindship*.

No, that is not a misprint. You may as well face it at once; Miss Jane Austen could speak French and read Italian, she could write English as no one has done before or since, but at one point her spelling was shaky. To the end of her days, when she had to write a word like *receive* or *believe* she was never quite sure which came first, the i or the e. When her novels came to be published the compositors could be relied on to straighten that out, but it will endear her to many of us to find, even in her later letters, *piece* appearing as *peice* and even when she was a multiple aunt, *niece* often as *neice*. When her little burlesque first saw print—more than a hundred years after it was written—no one could bear to change even a letter of it. *Love and Freindship* it remains to this day and I hope you will not be asked that word in a spelling match!

A lady named Isabel starts the burlesque by requiring from Laura an account of her Misfortunes and Adventures. Her friend declares that "never will I comply with your request till I may be no longer in danger from again experiencing such dreadful ones." Isabel thinks she might take a chance. "Surely that time is at hand. You are this day 55. If a woman may ever be said to be in safety from the determined perseverance of desperate lovers … surely it must be at such a time of life."

Laura herself is not sure she is as safe as all that, but without more delay plunges into the tale for the guidance of Isabel's young daughter.

It begins when an unknown young man bursts into the cottage of her parents: "The noble youth informed us that his name was Lindsay—for particular reasons, however, I shall conceal it under the name of Talbot."

He had left home in spirited protest against his father's suggestion that he might do worse than marry a certain young lady.

> "No never, exclaimed I! Lady Dorothea is lovely and
> engaging; I prefer no woman to her, but know Sir, that
> I scorn to marry her in compliance with your wishes.

No! Never shall it be said that I obliged my Father!"

We all admired the Noble Manliness of his reply.

So they were immediately married by her father, "who though he had never taken orders had been bred to the church," and at once set off to live with *his* father. This family, however, was lacking in finer feeling. His sister brought to Edward's attention that his father would have to support them.

"Support? What support will Laura want which she can receive from him?"

"Only those very insignificant ones of Victuals and Drink," answered she.

Does she imagine, he wants to know, that there is no other support for an exalted mind than "the mean and indelicate employment of Eating and Drinking?" "None that I know of so efficacious," his sister calmly replies. This is clearly no place for two young people of spirit. They go to the house of Edward's friend Augustus, where Laura meets Sophia his wife. The young men fly into each other's arms, the girls "faint alternately upon a sofa." Separated in consequence of Augustus's having "gracefully purloined a considerable sum of money," the quartette does not reassemble until the ladies come upon both gentlemen "insensible in the middle of a road, having been thrown out of a post-chaise." For an hour and a quarter the girls come out strong, "Sophia fainting every minute and I running mad as often." Finally Edward opens an eye, murmurs "Laura, I fear I have been overturned," and immediately expires.

Laura survives, but lying so long on the damp ground proves too much for Sophia. With her expiring breath she sums up the result of her experience:

> "My beloved Laura, take warning from my unhappy end and avoid the imprudent conduct which occasioned it … Beware of fainting fits … Though at the time they may be refreshing and agreeable, yet beleive [sic] me, they will in the end, if too often repeated, and at improper seasons, prove destructive to your Constitution. … A frenzy fit is not one quarter so pernicious; it is an exercise to the Body, and if not too violent, is I dare say conducive to health in consequence— Run mad as often as you chuse; but do not faint—"

With this advice, serious for all its smiles, Miss Jane

Austen, at fifteen, swept swoons clean out of her path as an author. If she should write—she must by this time have said to herself "when" instead of "if"—at least she knew what she would not write about. Perhaps—perhaps something might be done with a story about a real girl who took this sort of nonsense with a girl's seriousness—it might be amusing to see into what it might lead her! But that was vague as yet. There was time enough. *Northanger Abbey* was years ahead.

Love and Freindship belonged to the whole family at Steventon, but it was dedicated to someone outside: Mme. la Comtesse de Feuillide. Eliza might be worldly, she might enjoy the French fashions, but she had an English heart.

Chapter Nine

THE Rectory circle was widening, but the bond still held close. James married Anne Mathew, daughter of General and Lady Jane Mathew; Lady Jane was the daughter of a duke. Within three years Anne died, leaving one little daughter, and in time, his second wife was the daughter of a clergyman, Mary Lloyd, one of the Austen sisters' good friends.

Edward the Fortunate returned from his Grand Tour and made quite as fortunate a marriage; the lovely Elizabeth, daughter of Sir Brook Bridges, baronet, fully agreed with him that sharing one's happiness more than doubled it.

Eliza's widowhood had not lasted long. She was not made for sorrow. The world was still with her and London society still charming. She could still enjoy a whirlwind courtship and keep it whirling as long as possible, till she decided whether she could manage to "bring her mind to give up dear Liberty and yet dearer flirtation" in favor of marrying Henry Austen. She was in two minds about it, saying of herself that "after a few months stay in the country she sometimes thinks it possible to undertake sober matrimony, but a few weeks stay in London convinces her how little the state suits her taste." Henry, who had been briefly engaged to a young lady described as "a pretty, wicked-looking girl with bright black eyes which pierce through and through," was free again and renewed his siege of Eliza with vigor and persistance. She was ten years older than he, her French fortune was gone, she had a delicate little son to whom she was devoted; all these disadvantages she set before him faithfully and he resolutely pushed them aside. It took him some time to do so. It was three years before the little Comtesse married Henry in 1797 and became Eliza Austen. Handsomer than ever and just as unpredictable, Henry left off the scarlet coat of a Militia Officer, took her to London and became a banker.

Cassandra had entered on what promised to be a long engagement, though a happy, even-tempered one. Thomas Fowle, a curate of good family and not quite enough money for a prudent marriage, found that as an army chaplain in the West Indies he could make enough to return for a wedding; he set off and Cassandra set herself to fine sewing and practical interest in how a house should be run. There was no reason why she should stay at home from dances, and now that the elder sister was formally engaged, every reason why the younger should enter society at once. Miss Jane, who loved to dance, could do so to her heart's content. This was a fine district for it.

The Assemblies at Basingstoke were famous, the Rector kept a carriage and pair, and though seven miles each way was rather a pull, it need not be taken all at once. At Manydown Park the daughters of the house, two of Jane's greatest friends, would be going, too. When the Rectory wheels were heard crunching on the driveway, the girls would come running down the broad staircase in a flutter of welcomes, and the Rector's daughters would be transferred to their coach, taken to the ball and picked up at Manydown on the way home. It is never a long journey in a carriage packed with lighthearted girls who talk about a party all the way there and talk it over all the way back.

This was by no means the only great house where the Austen sisters could break the journey, or, for that matter, attend a private ball. Most of their acquaintance in the neighborhood had rooms large enough for a long line of couples to go through a set without having to dance through doorways. Ashe was the home of Jane's dear Mrs. Lefroy, her fellow-partisan of Mary, Queen of Scots, with whom there had always been the peculiarly pleasant bond that can exist between a bright child and an understanding adult; at Ashe the large folding-doors at the end of the dining parlor could be opened out into the room beyond and make them one. The Harwoods gave balls at Deane, at Hurstborne Park one was given annually by Lord Portsmouth who had been a pupil at Steventon Rectory, and at Kempshott House, where George, Prince of Wales, had lately been in residence, the present occupier gave one so elegant that dresses suitable for it offered young ladies noted for pretty clothes—like Miss J. Austen—days of delicious anxiety.

To Jane, a ball was a good thing from the moment the invitation came. It was good to be assured, by a last look at someone else's impartial mirror, that one's dress was right, shoe-roses in place, scarf floating with the proper unstudied elegance and one's self in good looks. Jane herself believed none of that talk about the Austen sisters being "perfect beauties" and "breaking hearts by dozens," but as she went by a looking-glass on the way down to the dance, the consciousness that she was looking well made her look even better. The little Countess in her great hoop at the Court of

France, with her diamonds and high-piled powdered head, had never been happier or prettier than slender Jane, in India muslin, her brown hair curling naturally round rosy cheeks, the "hind hair" tucked up under one of the charming caps or turbans ladies wore at evening parties. When Frank, one of the "sailor brothers," won his first prize-money at sea, he spent a good part of it on topaz crosses, one for each of his sisters, to wear with pretty dresses.

It was good to feel sure, when the curtseys and introductions of the first "great circle" were over and the violins began tuning in the ballroom, that at least one and usually several gentlemen would come with no reluctant step to lead her to the set. It was exhilarating to see the line of couples lengthening and know it would be a good ball. Jane wrote to Cassandra, away on a visit, that there had been twenty dances and that she had danced them all without fatigue. "With a few couples I fancy I could just as well dance for a week together as for half an hour," said Miss Jane Austen, who might be slender but was certainly robust.

For this was strenuous dancing, moving swiftly for all its elegance and grace. Not the minuet now, as it had been when Beau Nash ruled fashion in Bath. Theoretically the minuet was still part of a young lady's education—five pounds five it cost to learn it at a fashionable dancing school —but for practical purposes its solemn parade had passed. When you said dance now, you meant a country-dance.

Do not be misled by that name to think there was anything countrified about it. The word was derived from *contredanse* and it was an elegant entertainment, involving figures that could be almost indefinitely varied, though its basic plan was on the lines of the Roger de Coverley that sent so many of our American ancestors up and down the middle. A young girl's ball-dress stood out a little at the hem for greater freedom of movement; it showed her low-heeled satin slippers as they glided through the steps—for a lady who danced must above all be graceful. She must glide, not jump. In particular, her step must be elastic—the low heels helped for that—and if it was sometimes so elastic that she bounced, that was a fault readily forgiven to the young, healthy and happy. This happy, healthy Jane who was good at anything requiring delicacy and accuracy, from cup-and-ball and exquisite tambour work to the intricacies of this new French dance called "The Baker's Wife," looked forward to a ball as an experience in bliss.

It was not necessary to this emotion that she should know herself to be the belle of the ball. It was not even necessary that it should be a very good ball. "There were more danc-ers than the room would hold," she wrote to Cassandra, "which is enough to constitute a good ball at any time." Two years later she danced nine out of twelve dances and was "merely prevented from dancing the rest by the absence of a partner." She reported, with the devastating frankness girls usually reserve for other girls, whenever her own tri-umph had been less than complete. Those bright eyes were not looking for conquests to the exclusion of everything else. A gentleman's heart was quite safe with her and she was not carried away by the attention of a gentleman who had no intentions. Flirtation belonged to a ball if you were young and pretty; she was not one of those to whom a ball would be rather a punishment than a pleasure. In one of her novels * an affected young woman protests, "I should like balls infinitely better if they were carried on in a different manner; but there is something insufferably tedious in the usual process of such a meeting. It would surely be much more rational if conversation instead of dancing made the order of the day." To which her brother replies, "Much more rational, my dear Caroline, I dare say, but it would not be near so much like a ball."

Partners might come or go with Jane's good will; a life partner would be another matter. Thus in this lighthearted season Tom Lefroy was great fun. He was the nephew of her dear Mrs. Lefroy, which was in his favor—but then he *would* wear a white coat to look like the hero of Fielding's *Tom Jones*, which was against him. The younger Miss Austen's heart, unlike that of the elder, was by no means fixed as yet; she liked nothing better than the decorous coquetry, the sort of give-and-take that is to love-making what pat-ball

* *Pride and Prejudice*

is to tennis, and Tom Lefroy could keep the ball in the air as skilfully as she could. The miniature that shows how he looked at twenty proves that he must have radiated charm. But for one whose preference for Jane was so marked that everybody in the neighborhood found it amusing, for a youth so clearly on the very verge of proposing, Jane was amused to find how easily she could deflect that purpose. "He has been so excessively laughed at about me at Ashe that he is ashamed of coming to Steventon." Instead, he went to Ireland and in time married there—and when he was an old man told his son that he had really loved her dearly and that no one who had ever known her could ever forget her.

Jane herself took his departure no more seriously than she had taken him. Cassandra evidently thought she was giving the charming Tom more encouragement than she intended, for Jane wrote back :

> You scold me so much in the nice long letter which I have this moment received from you that I am almost afraid to tell you how my Irish friend and I behaved. Imagine to yourself everything most profligate and shocking in the way of dancing and sitting down to-gether. I *can* expose myself, however, only *once more,* because he leaves the country soon after next Friday, on which we *are* to have a dance at Ashe, after all.

And in her next:

> At length the day the day is come on which I am to flirt my last with Tom Lefroy, and when you receive this it will be over. My tears flow as I write at the melancholy idea.

Then there was a Mr. B. who did not even try to forget the time he came into the neighborhood from the University in the Christmas holidays, and wrote back to his hostess that it would give him particular pleasure to have an opportunity of improving his acquaintance with the Austen family "with a hope of creating a nearer interest." That suited Jane well enough, especially as he did not come any nearer.

> There appears less love and more sense in it than sometimes appeared before. It will all go on exceedingly

well, and decline away in a very reasonable manner. Our indifference will soon be mutual, unless his regard, which appeared to spring from knowing nothing about me at first, is best supported by never seeing me.

Yet it was some years later before Mr. B. married a young lady from Antigua, and Jane, who had never seen the bride, rather preferred her to be

of a silent turn and rather ignorant, but naturally

ignorant and wishing to learn, fond of cold veal pies, green tea in the afternoon and a green window-blind at night.

From which one gets some idea of what Mr. B. was like.

No, neither of these was the man. Jane had not seen him yet and was quite willing to wait until he appeared. But she would not consider a substitute.

Certainly not when there was so much more in life even than dancing or flirting. In the brown dressing room upstairs where the sisters could talk or keep the companionable silences that mean that someone is writing, in the downstairs sitting room with a bit of sewing ready to draw over the small sheets of paper should a neighbor come in, people were coming to life under that clear, delicate hand. There would be no more burlesques, no more parodies. Jane Austen, not yet twenty-one, was creating on her own account.

Chapter Ten

*E*LINOR AND MARIANNE it was called, and it was
to be a full-length novel in the form of letters. In such
form, novels of social life were usually written—Miss Burney's *Evelina*, for instance. Jane herself hardly knew when
it had begun to take shape in her mind, and she was by no
means sure that it had taken the right shape. Letters were
all very well for a burlesque such as *Love and Freindship*, but
this was to be a story about two sisters, young, unmarried,
living in the same house in the country; why should they be
writing letters to each other if they lived at home and were
never separated? Jane rapidly brought *Elinor and Marianne*
to a close and laid it aside. She might come back to it later.
It had good material. It might make a good novel if it could
be given the right shape.

Meanwhile, something else was coming to life and making its own shape—coming so fast she could hardly keep up
with it on paper. She smiled as she wrote it and whenever
she thought of it she smiled. No one outside the family knew
that she was writing at all, but inside the family it was one
of those secrets everybody knows. Even the littlest niece,
keeping close to Aunt Jane for the love she always found

there, knew that something unusually exciting was going on. The little creature had the run of the room upstairs where her young aunts kept their personal treasures; Jane's piano was there with the book of songs she had copied out—she loved to sing but had so poor an opinion of her own voice that she sang only before breakfast with the door closed. Cassandra's drawing materials were there, and the painted press with their pretty clothes in it, and their own particular books on shelves above. The table was there on which stood the little mahogany box-desk that belonged to Jane. Sometimes in the midst of their play Aunt Jane would begin to laugh softly, run to the little desk, write something quickly down and come back laughing. Sometimes she would go on writing for what seemed a long time. Sometimes she would call Aunt Cassy and read her something she had just put on paper; every now and then she would have to stop to let Aunt Cassy laugh and the two would laugh together. She was telling Aunt Cassy about people the little girl had never seen, and the child was too young to understand what they were doing, but she heard their names so often she came to know them as well as her own. Sometimes she herself spoke of Elizabeth Bennet and Mr. Darcy downstairs. Indeed, she did it so often the sisters explained to her that they were a secret no one but the family so much as guessed—so, of course, she wouldn't speak of them outside the family ?

And she never did till years after, and when just about everyone who read English had heard about the book in which these people were to be found.

Not, of course, under the title it bore when Jane first wrote it. Then she called it *First Impressions*.

Now we know it as *Pride and Prejudice*.

Even when the manuscript reached its last page and had all been read aloud, its very existence remained a closely guarded family secret. Outside that circle no one had an idea that the Rector's younger daughter had written a real book. It showed how well the Austen clan held together that such a secret could be kept so long inside, with not a breath of it getting out, considering how many insiders read it from first word to last. Moreover, they kept on reading it more than once. When Cassandra at Edward's asked for another look at the manuscript, Jane wrote back: "I do not wonder at your wanting to read *First Impressions* again, so seldom as you have gone through it, and that so long ago!" Six months later, when another member of the clan asked for one more chance at the script, Jane sent Cassandra a laughing message for transmission: "I would not let Martha read *First Impressions* again upon any account, and am very glad that I did not leave it in your power. She is very cunning, but I saw through her design; she means to publish it from memory, and one more perusal must enable her to do it!"

Young as the book was, without even a permanent title, no more than the shape of things to come, it was already showing something just as true of it today—whoever reads it once reads it again, and the more nearly he knows it by heart the more often he reads it.

The Rector, on first reading, thought it quite good enough to print exactly as it was. So on November 1,1797, just short of Jane's twenty-second birthday, Messrs. Cadell, the publishers, received what was probably the most unbusinesslike letter to come their way that year. The Rector had in his possession, he informed them courteously, "a manuscript novel, comprising three volumes, about the length of Miss Burney's *Evelina*." He knew how important it was that such a work "should make its first appearance under a respectable name," so he applied to Messrs. Cadell and would be much obliged "if you will inform me whether you choose to be concerned in it."

Just how Cadell was to be concerned seemed a little vague in the Rector's mind. What, he asked, would be the expense of publishing it at the author's own risk and what would Cadell venture to advance for the property of it, if on perusal it is approved of? In this polite obscurity as to whether he expected the author to pay or be paid, he courteously concludes, "Should you give any encouragement, I will send you the work."

In these days of literary agents and advance publicity, it may be hard to believe that anyone could expect encouragement from a publisher who had not been given the name of the book, a word of what it was about, the faintest idea of who might be likely to read it, or even the name of the author, though this last was not surprising, as the author had no intention of having her name mentioned at all. Naturally the publisher indicated by return mail that he did not choose to be concerned.

Nobody's feelings were hurt. You could not call this a rejection; there had been no offer. The Rector had murmured something about a manuscript and publishers have ways of letting it be known that they are not interested. Jane's "darling child" had not been insulted. It had not even been mentioned.

Jane herself was rather relieved than otherwise. The story had almost told itself, but already she could see how it could be told better. Now she could make those improvements before this dear manuscript should be irrevocably fixed in type. Even the title was not yet quite what it should be. It would be what she called her "private regale" to keep going over the whole thing, putting it aside at intervals and bringing it out again until it should be as nearly perfect as she could make it, before she could say good-bye to the Bennet family, to Mr. Collins, Darcy, Wickham, Bingley—all these alluring people, and send them out into the world.

We do not know just what *First Impressions* was like when it was made ready to send to Cadell. We cannot compare it with what it became, because every time Jane made a revised copy she destroyed the one before it. As it was sixteen years before it finally came out as *Pride and Prejudice*, she may have made several such revisions, not verbal only, but in the choice of incidents to show, in action, just what these people really are, so you would recognize them today should you meet them at a party. Somewhere along these years she found the perfect title in capital letters at the close of Miss Burney's *Cecilia*, when the troubles of its hero and heroine are ended by their coming to understand each other and it is said of their misunderstandings that "the whole of this unfortunate business has been the result of PRIDE AND PREJUDICE." But whatever Jane Austen's book was at the beginning, it had the freshness, the gaiety, the charm of youth—and keeps them now. Its heart is that of a twenty-year-old.

Such revisions take place so often in Jane Austen's life that one who tells its story must keep moving forward and back, if any light is to be thrown on what we want most to know—how she wrote her books. They did not come into full existence all at once, in a single burst of creative energy that took her away from all other activities until it had produced a masterpiece. Sometimes she had two or more novels going on at once, in various stages of preparation.

Meanwhile, the everyday occupations of a clergyman's daughter, the preoccupations of a pretty young lady moving in good society, went on. She herself might have a low opinion of flannel as a fabric and think it so base an article that its being comparatively good or bad was of little importance, but old women in the cottages who expected flannel petticoats and woollen stockings were not disappointed.

When Cassandra was away from home Jane kept house. "I am very grand indeed," she reported; "I carry about the keys … and twice since I began this letter have had orders to give in the kitchen. …" "My mother desires me to tell you that I am a very good housekeeper, which I have no reluctance in doing, because I really think it my peculiar excellence, and for this reason—I always take care to provide such things as please my own appetite, which I consider the chief merit in housekeeping." Her letters to her sister dance through details of home dinners; one was "very good yesterday, and the chicken boiled perfectly tender; therefore," says Miss Jane with a chuckle, "I shall not be obliged to dismiss Nanny on that account."

These charming gowns, too; they called for thought, and so did their upkeep. "I am sorry to say that my new colored gown is very much washed out, though I charged everybody to take great care of it. I hope yours is so too," adds the irrepressible Jane, who wrote just as she talked whenever she wrote to the sister who would know just what she meant. Those evening caps that young ladies wore at parties—now, there was something that called not only for fashion but for originality, and if one's own resources were limited, for co-operation with other members of the family. One cap in which Jane was much admired at an important ball began with a black velvet ruffle borrowed from Cassandra, who was away from home at the time. Another had narrow silver ribbon twice round the crown, without any bow and a little feather standing up at the side. Miss Jane Austen was partial—in moderation—to the color called *coquelicot*, a lively pink as pretty as its name, and though she would not think of having a whole dress of it, knew how much a touch of it in the right spot—over the left ear, for instance—could do for the success of a headdress, especially if the eyes beneath it, hazel in the daytime, grew dark as their pupils widened in the excitement of the dance.

Besides, she had other forms of fine sewing. "We are very busy making Edward's shirts and I am proud to say I am the neatest worker of the party." One can well believe it who has seen at Chawton Cottage a piece of her embroidery exquisitely fine, especially as a good part of it must have been made by candlelight by one whose eyes were never very strong. "I use them as little as I can," she protested in one of those intervals when they were especially weak, "but *you* know, and *Elizabeth* knows, and everybody who had weak

eyes knows, how delightful it is to hurt them by employment, against the advice and entreaty of all one's friends."

Cassandra, too, was sewing busily. Her wedding clothes were not far from ready when a letter came from Antigua that put them all away. Yellow fever, as yet unchecked in the Caribbees, had laid hold of young Thomas Fowle. Without warning, she learned that the boy whom first she had met as a pupil in her father's house, the betrothed who had gone to the West Indies to earn enough to marry on, was dead.

Lord Craven, who had appointed him as chaplain, was wild with self-reproach. Had he but known that the young man was engaged to be married, he would never have taken him to so deadly a climate. But young Fowle, rather than seem to ask for special consideration, had not told him. His will came back, a last message. He had left Cassandra a thousand pounds.

No letter remains from this period. In these months Jane and Cassandra were never separated. No sounds of grief came from the little room lately brimming with laughter, but there were the silences that speak of sorrow borne together. The old prediction for Cassy had come true; Jane had "insisted on sharing her fate." From henceforth they would never be divided.

There is something to be said for good manners in bearing grief, and while the eighteenth century was still in the air, good manners among the gentry kept a lady from darkening the lives of others with sorrow that could not be helped this side of Heaven. Cassandra, who had worn such delicate colors, put on black, but she wore it gracefully. Without tears, without words, something told her friends that she would always wear it in her heart.

But that would be far in the future. The sisters now had only just grown up. They were young, but they were young women.

Chapter Eleven

YOUNG women? They were more. They were Elegant Young Women. Even Aunt Leigh Perrot, who moved in the best society and had ninety guests at her card parties, called them that, and she was one to make a little praise go a long way. Besides, she said it under circumstances that did her credit. She was in jail at the time, and when her husband's sister, the Rector's wife, who like everyone else was outraged at the very idea of her being arrested, offered to send Cassandra and Jane to stay with her till she should be freed, Mrs. Leigh Perrot stoutly refused to let "those Elegant Young Women" be Inmates of a Prison or subject to its Inconveniences. Jane and Cassandra, prepared to go, paused at this refusal, perhaps the more willingly because to be in the same house with Aunt Perrot, let alone the same jail, would not be exactly exhilarating. She had all the virtues and practically none of the softer graces. Everyone respected her but nobody liked her very much, except her husband who loved her dearly and to whom she was devoted. It was indeed the happiest of marriages and long had been; now in the Indian Summer of his retirement to Bath, the most fashionable place in which to have the gout, they were seldom out of each other's sight.

It was for a few moments only, on their way to drink the waters one early afternoon in August, that Mrs. Leigh Perrot left him to do a little shopping. Bath today is still full of tempting little shops; it was then a center of fashion, getting all the new modes from London as fast as they came down, and Mrs. Leigh Perrot, who needed black lace, bought some at Miss Gregory's millinery establishment, paid for it, received her change and the little packet and rejoined her husband. Coming back the same way, the shopkeeper came out and asked if there were not also some white lace in the packet. Aunt Perrot, mystified, handed it over unopened—and there, inside the black lace, was a card of white. Probably saying a sharp word about some people's carelessness in doing up bundles, Aunt Perrot went on and thought no more about it till an impertinent unsigned note arrived for "Mrs. Leigh Perrot, Lace Dealer," asking about "the piece of lace stolen from Bath Street a few days ago." It was followed, to her horror and amaze, by a constable with a warrant for her immediate appearance before the Mayor. The Perrots both went straightway; there were the two shop-people, one of whom swore to seeing her take the lace, the other to finding it in her possession. The Mayor did not in the least want to commit Mrs. Perrot for trial; nobody believed a word of the charge, but it had been made. Aunt Perrot, sternly refusing bail, went to prison and her devoted husband went, too. *The Times* noted discreetly that "the Lady of a Gentleman at Bath, possessed of a good fortune, and respected by a numerous circle of acquaintances, was committed on Thursday by G. Chapman esq., the Mayor, to the county gaol at Ilchester, on a charge of privately stealing a card of lace from a haberdasher's shop." As she vigorously

refused to come out of "gaol" till she had been brought to trial, the Perrots both stayed in for seven months.

Long before that the shopkeepers would have been glad enough to let the whole thing drop. Apparently they had been trying to frighten a rich woman into paying them enough to stave off their impending bankruptcy, but Aunt Perrot was the wrong rich woman to select. Nobility and gentry, relatives and friends, came forward to declare that she could not possibly have done any such thing. One look at her unbending portrait tells us even now that they were right. She made a ringing speech in court; her just indignation swept the evidence to a triumphant acquittal. She left the courtroom with not a stain on her character and went straight back to the same numerous circle of acquaintance with even more respect from them. The case had cost her husband nearer two than a thousand pounds; the jailor's family, with whom they took their meals, meant well, but their table manners hardly bear mentioning—though in her letters Aunt Perrot mentioned them in detail—and the jailor's children clambered over his gouty knees. Still his sweet disposition stood the strain and at last, when the moment of his wife's vindication came, he was so happy that they both were happy ever after.

It was one of those flashes of melodrama that played along the edges of Jane's quiet experience. This one came nearer than the edge. In the book that Sir Frank Douglas MacKinnon wrote about the case,* he calls attention to a letter that shows how she could have been innocently mixed up in it. Less than two months before, Jane, on a visit to "My Aunt," had written from Bath that she had seen "some gauzes in a shop on Bath Street yesterday at only 4s. a yard, but they were not so good or so pretty as mine.... My Aunt told me of a very cheap shop near Walcot Church, to which I shall go in quest of something for you." And he muses, "I cannot resist the temptation to speculate. Was the shop in Bath Street Miss Gregory's? And if Mrs. Leigh Perrot was right in thinking she was the victim of a plot there, just over two months later, is it possible that, if Jane Austen had been tempted to buy some of the gauzes at four shillings a

---

* Grand Larceny, being the trial of Jane Leigh Perrot, aunt of Jane Austen, Oxford University Press. 132 pp., 1937.

yard, she might have had an extra length put in her parcel, and then have been charged with stealing it?"

The sisters offered to sit with Mrs. Leigh Perrot in court, but My Aunt would not hear of it— "To have two Young Creatures gazed at in a public Courtroom would cut me to the very heart"—and so Jane, who had nerved herself for the ordeal, thankfully escaped it.

The family at home was smaller now, but there were new homes in the family for the sisters to visit. James had married again; his wife was Mary, the sister of Martha Lloyd, his own sisters' dear friend. Henry and Eliza were enjoying high life in London, going to parties and giving them; Jane had written blithely from London that she was "once more in this scene of dissipation and vice, and I begin already to feel my morals corrupted." For all the regiment of nurses and maids surrounding the rapidly rising family of Edward and Elizabeth, Cassandra was constantly and affectionately in demand there. Frank and Charles were at sea, rapidly rising in their profession, though at first Jane found how trying it was to wait for news of their promotion. When news of Frank's did come she dashed it off to Cassandra all in a breath, winding up with, "There! I may now finish my letter and go and hang myself, for I am sure I can neither write nor do anything which will not appear insipid to you after this."

Together or apart, there were cheerful trips to be made not too far from Steventon for comfortable travel in the family carriage. The Rector's horses were also used on the farm, but like those of Mr. Bennet in *Pride and Prejudice*, they were probably wanted on the farm more often than he could get them.

One day in November, 1800, Jane and her friend Martha were coming home from one of these carriage trips. It was good to see the friendly familiar house come in sight down the long village street. There was a special soft excitement in the moment, however often it happened. Going away was good but coming home was better.

Then came the surprise.

Mrs. Austen met them at the door, brimful of news. "Well, girls!" she cried. "It is all settled. We have decided to leave Steventon and go to Bath."

Neither of them could say a word. The shock took their breath away.

And the robust Miss Jane Austen, who had made such fine fun of fainting ladies, for the first and only time in her life fainted dead away.

Chapter Twelve

ONE way to recover from a shock is to face up to it. It is also a typically English way, and Jane took it. Everything had indeed been settled. The Rector's habit had always been to take plenty of time to make up his mind, but once made up, to act quickly and completely. Though the news came upon Jane as if the floor had suddenly dropped out, husband and wife had been for some time considering the move.

They were all to leave the house where Jane had been born, the landscape whose every line—rolling meadows, softly rising hills, blossoming hedgerows—had been part of her for the first twenty-four years of her life. The barn with its glamorous memories would be itself a memory. The dressing room on the floor over the entrance, where the first impressions of Elizabeth Bennet and Fitzwilliam Darcy had kept Cassandra laughing—Jane realized that she had a heartstring round every doorknob, now that they were to be torn away.

But supposing the family were ever to move, this would be the right time to do so; it had so much reason that Jane, who was above all a reasonable creature with a genius for understanding other people, could not help seeing that it was. Her father had not married very young and she was near the last of a large family. He was a vigorous seventy, ready to retire and let James take his place, which James was ready and willing to do. The ladies of the Rectory felt that James's wife had been willing for some little time. It would be better all round, instead of staying there and taking on a married son as assistant, to go clean away and leave the newcomers unimpeded by advice. Mrs. Austen felt she might give some if she stayed. They could count on nearly six hundred pounds a year; on that they could keep house comfortably, with cook, housemaid and manservant, in a cheerful place where there would be people coming and going to make it lively, but where they already would have friends among the best people who stayed.

To all this Jane agreed. Packing for a complete removal, which set in at once, took her mind off her emotions. There were more than five hundred books of her father's to be disposed of and some of her own; everyone who loves books and has to move quantities of them knows that some must be taken along, whatever else goes, and such books went with them, but transport by wagon was too expensive to take them all, or much of the furniture. Jane's pianoforte at the sale brought about what she had expected; her books, as they always do, rather less. Certain favorite pieces were settled in the family. Cassandra, who was with Edward's family during these transactions, thought Jane might leave that cabinet of hers to Anna, who had played in that room when Darcy and Elizabeth were setting out towards literature.

But Jane replied: "You are very kind in planning presents for me to make, and my Mother has shown me exactly the same attention—but as I do not choose to have Generosity

dictated to me, I shall not resolve on giving my cabinet to Anna till the first thought of it has been my own" —a touch of spice that will be savored by anyone who has been told by others what to give away and to whom.

With all this going on at once, Jane was getting more and more reconciled to the idea of removal. "We have lived long enough in this Neighborhood, the Basingstoke Balls are certainly on the decline, there is something interesting in the bustle of going away, and the prospect of spending future summers by the sea or in Wales is very delightful." To one of her disposition, making the best of things always made them better. When she set out for a ball she always expected to have a good time and had it. As she said herself, she was "not one who thought it worth while to wait for enjoyment until there is some real opportunity for it." There would be opportunities on ahead. Another house was waiting, chosen after careful househunting, at Number 4 Sidney Place in Bath, not too far from—but not too near—the somewhat dictatorial kindness of Aunt Perrot.

The last of the packing completed, the last farewell visits made and received, it was with no uncertain step that Jane mounted the chaise, gave one last, long, loving look to the house that had been the center of her world, drew the curtain on Steventon, set out for Bath, and, save for occasional visits, never came back.

But because she had lived there for half her life—from the moment that eyes, senses, mind began to take in, unconsciously and surely, the memories that longest remain —what she took away with her remains for us today. Do not look for the Rectory when now you visit Steventon. All you will see where once it stood is a grassy meadow sloping gently to a bank not too steep to roll down, and

in the midst of the meadow an iron pump from which the Austens got their water. A low fence surrounds this now; it stood then in the washhouse back of the parsonage and there was a well under it. The sturdy old house, meant for a large family to grow up in, was too plain for later taste; it was pulled down and another with more style built on the hillside that overlooks the meadow. This is still called the New Parsonage ; the people who live there were very courteous in pointing out the pump, but the parsonage house is now in North Waltham, further up the road. It was the vicar there who saw that the small parish church of St. Nicholas, half a mile along the track that runs by the east side of the Rectory field at Steventon, was opened for me to see the

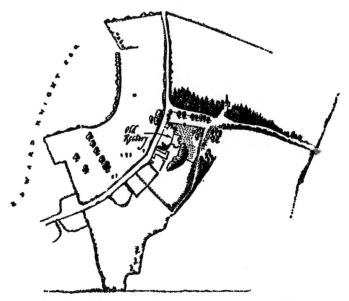

Register Book with young Jane's improvements. It was one of his churchwardens who brought from his own house a framed and glazed *Plan of Steventon in the County of Hants, showing the Original Glebe*, on which are put down, as if looking from the hillside, the fields, the trees, the meadows, the outline of the Old Rectory, still standing when the map was drawn in 1821.

Yet nowhere in England can a lover of Jane Austen find himself more at home than here. The last of the elms round the Rectory crashed in a gale before she left, but tall elms still stand. In spring, primroses, hyacinths and violets still blossom under the hedges. Here is still the soft landscape her last look took away with her. In the manuscripts steadily gathering in the little desk, what she learned there was steadily being transmuted into literature.

And all unknown to her, the great year of her life, the hidden year, was fast approaching.

Chapter Thirteen

ONE of the reasons Jane had given herself for the re-moval had been that now there would be "the prospect of spending the summers by the sea." The very thought of the sea, inland though she was, had always been dear to Jane. Every letter from her sailor brothers brought it nearer; she looked up the name of every ship on her own Navy List. When Charles had sent each of his sisters a topaz cross on a gold chain, she held the sea in her hand. Now she would be able to see it, even to be, for not too long at a time, part of it. Since royalty had found how pleasant sea-bathing could be at the fishing village of Brighthelmstone, and Brighton had risen around it, inland watering places had begun to lose their popularity and villages along the coast, loved by a few, had begun to think of attracting the many.

It was on one of the visits whose prospects now had opened—at Sidmouth perhaps, or somewhere else in that dreamlike Devonshire summer—that Jane Austen's life came to flower. She knew that she had met the man she loved and that he loved her.

They scarcely put it into words, even to each other. It was enough, in those few days when time stood still, to know that they had found each other. We would not know that even now, had not Cassandra, years after, been so moved by hearing of something that reminded her of those days that she suddenly threw off her long reserve and spoke to her niece of them. While Cassandra and Jane were making a long, leisurely tour of Devonshire, stopping at pleasant places, they had met a young clergyman, visiting his brother who was one of the doctors of the locality. It was clear that at first sight he and Jane had fallen in love. Cassandra thought him "one of the most charming persons she had ever known," worthy even of her adored Jane, and Cassandra, who seldom admired a stranger, would be especially exacting where Jane's future would be concerned. When the sisters went on, the young clergyman asked permission to join them later in their tour. Arrangements for life were a formal matter then: permission was given with a tacit understanding of all it meant, and a meeting place appointed. When the sisters arrived there, a letter was handed them, announcing his death.

Like Cassandra's dream of the future, Jane's had passed. The girl who had flirted so gaily with charming young men and held them off so considerately that to the end of their days they would remember her with affection, had fallen in love as swiftly as Shakespeare's Juliet. But though her love affair was just as sudden and just as soon closed by death, it was not "too rash, too ill-advised" to escape from the keeping of her own heart. No one knows his name. Endless conjecture has not found him in her novels. All we know of the hero of her "nameless, dateless" romance, is that he loved Jane Austen—and that she loved him.

Perhaps an echo of it comes at the climax of the last novel she was to write. She had finished *Persuasion*; it was ready for the press. The crescendo of its later chapters, steadily quickening in intensity, had reached its highest point. The long separation of Wentworth and Anne had ended. But Jane, whose powers were now at their height, was herself deeply depressed in spirit. The chapter with the climax was not what it should be. Something in it should be glorious, something should ring from the very depths of the heart. She could not sleep. Next day she canceled the chapter and writing in a glow, achieved perfection. Wentworth overhears a conversation that turns on whether it is more man's nature than woman's to forget those they have loved. And at its height he hears:

"Oh!" cried Anne eagerly, "I hope I do justice to all that is felt by you, and by those who resemble you. God forbid that I should undervalue the warm and faithful feelings of any of my fellow-creatures. I should deserve utter contempt if I dared to suppose that true attachment and constancy were known only by woman. No, I believe you capable of everything great and good in your married lives. I believe you equal to every important exertion, and to every domestic forbearance, so long as—if I may be allowed the expression, so long as you have an object. I mean, while the woman you love lives, and lives for you. All the privilege I claim for my own sex (it is not a very enviable one, you need not covet it) is that of loving longest, when existence or when hope is gone."

She could not immediately have uttered another sentence; her heart was too full, her breath too much oppressed.

Something rings from a full heart in Anne's last sentence, something from unforgotten experience.

Chapter Fourteen

IT was on another of these little journeys out of Bath that something serio-comic did take place—far from comic to Jane—that indirectly throws some light on that experience. For once in her life Jane took herself so completely by surprise that it threw her off her balance.

She had come with Cassandra from their new home to visit James and Mary at the old Rectory and spend some of the time with friends round about who had missed them. Two of these friends were at Manydown Park, the great house where Jane used to break the journey to and from a Basingstoke Ball, meet its daughters Catherine and Alethea Bigg, and stay the night. The Austen sisters were expected there now, to spend several days. But early in the morning of the day after they had set out, James and Mary heard hoofs clattering on the gravel and the roll of a carriage at speed. Hastening to the door, they saw the Manydown carriage rapidly approaching with all four girls, evidently in agitation. It drew up before the entrance. There they parted, without words but with tears and close embraces; then the girls from Manydown drove rapidly away and Cassandra, to whom Jane was clinging, led her through the door and still

without speaking, past James and Mary and up the stairs into their own room.

James and his wife looked at each other in amazement. Nothing like that had happened in the family before, least of all to even-tempered Jane, who was evidently the center of the commotion. Not till Cassandra came down did they learn what had happened. Catherine and Alethea had met them as rapturously as in their dancing days. The same laughter had been tossed back and forth as they dressed for dinner. At this the gaiety was all the greater for the months of separation, and their brother Harris was there to share it. Afterwards Cassandra, tired from the journey, left the drawing room and was soon fast asleep. Sometime in the night she was awakened. Beside her bed stood Jane, trembling, pale, too thoroughly upset to tell her at first what had upset her. Cassandra held her close and waited to hear. When the girls had been about to leave the drawing room their brother, who had evidently made with them some hopeful, happy arrangement, found an excuse to delay Jane's withdrawal. As soon as they were alone together, he had made her a formal proposal of marriage. And Jane had accepted him.

There was every reason, one might say, why she should have done so. He was young, not unpleasing, and evidently fond of her. Born to a handsome fortune, he had inherited another. This marriage would bring her back to the countryside she loved, her dear elder brother, the circle of life-long friends. Catherine and Alethea were at that moment holding their breaths upstairs in the hope that she would say "Yes" and become their sister. Jane said "Yes" and gave him her hand. Young Harris, somewhat dazed by the sudden flowering of his hope, watched her go lightly, smiling, up the stair.

And then, alone in her room with the candle out, the curly hair tucked under a nightcap, the most unreasonable wave of utter panic rose to take possession of the reasonable Jane. What, oh what, had she said? What was this she had done? She respected him, admired him—everything but love him. How could she ever, ever have accepted him? More terror-stricken by the moment, she groped through the dark to rouse Cassandra. They could not, must not stay. At the first ray of light the horses must be harnessed. At dawn Alethea and Catherine were awakened. Jane was too plainly suffering to be reasoned with. Clustering round her, the three shepherded her into the family carriage and took their own places there. The horses could not go fast enough....

James and Mary realized that to come back at once to the Rectory had been the only thing to do in such a complication. But when they found that James's own horses must be brought out at once and the sisters set on their way back to Bath, they realized how serious the matter must be to Jane. For James would not think of letting the two young ladies go unaccompanied; it was Friday; it would be hard to find, in so short a time, anyone to take his place in church on Sunday. But when Jane, who knew just how hard it would be, considerate Jane who never gave trouble, would not consent to a day's, an hour's delay, James knew what perturbation of spirit must now be driving her. Home alone could cure it. He took her home, and it did.

But Jane had found that however sensible, however handsome an establishment might be, she could not marry for an establishment.

Chapter Fifteen

IN those early years of the nineteenth century the nation was bracing itself for trouble and getting it. Napoleon's flotilla was making ready for the invasion of England and the British fleet was making sure he should do no such thing. News came in on every packet, thrilling to anyone with two brothers in action with the Royal Navy. History was rapidly working up to the day when England was to learn, all in one breath, that Trafalgar had been won and Nelson lost.

In the midst of all this, Jane finished another novel and sold it to a publisher.

Not a breath of these heroic, historic adventures touched its heroine, who was seventeen and living comfortably in the country when she was invited to spend six weeks at Bath and her own adventures began. But it was a long time before anyone but the Austens knew anything about them. The publisher who paid ten pounds for the manuscript and said he would bring it out, did not say when he would, and did not do so at all. Some years later, Henry, acting for the author whose name had not appeared in the transaction, bought back the manuscript for the same sum and then had the pleasure of telling the publisher that the "Lady" who had

written it was the author of two novels everybody was reading. But *Northanger Abbey*, as we know it now, was written
in those agitated years of which they show no trace.

It was at the height of the season when Catherine Morland, *Northanger Abbey*'s heroine, went to Bath, the capital
of fashion. *Northanger Abbey*, like *Evelina*, concerns a young
lady's first contact with the great world, but her adventures
were amusingly different from those of Miss Burney's heroine. The rage for "horrid" novels like *Mysteries of Udolpho*
had passed, but they still were being read and Catherine
Morland had read a good many. It had been about her only
excitement in the country. To be sure, their horrors usually
took place at some distance—such as the South of France,
where anything might be expected—but young Catherine
had the sort of half-belief that they might happen elsewhere

that does one no good in the South of England. It did her no harm, though in the process of getting some sense she stirred up a narrow escape of her own. But that is not why so many of us have read *Northanger Abbey* so often that we could find our way around Bath without a map—up and down Milsom Street where one of the shopwindows had a hat trimmed with *coquelicot* ribbons; in and out of the Pump Room where the favorite place of that resolute coquette Isabella Thorpe was on a bench with a view of both doors because it was "so out of the way"; up Beechen Cliff where the Tilneys, brother and sister, viewed the landscape with the eyes of persons accustomed to drawing and Catherine, who could not draw but was falling in love with Henry Tilney, learned so much on the way up about the principles of taste that at the top she "voluntarily rejected the whole city of Bath as unworthy to make part of a landscape." The charm of the book is that everything in it comes to us as it came to Catherine herself—through the eyes of an ingenuous young girl, seeing Bath for the first time and finding it wonderful, finding the world wonderful because for the first time she had fallen in love. In those few weeks she stayed seventeen but came of age. Whatever happens in them she would never forget and we, who live them along with her, always remember.

You can see the smile on Jane's face as she remembers the heroines of the Minerva Press Novels and describes her own heroine's first appearance in Society. Mr. Allen, her host, has just rejoined the ladies after playing cards: *

"Well, Miss Morland," said he directly. "I hope you have had an agreeable ball."

* *Chap. II, Northanger Abbey.*

"Very agreeable, indeed," she replied, vainly endeavouring to hide a great yawn.

"I wish she had been able to dance," said his wife; "I wish we could have got a partner for her. I have been saying how glad I should be if the Skinners were here this winter instead of last; or if the Parrys had come, as they talked of once, she might have danced with George Parry. I am sorry she has not had a partner."

...The company began to disperse when the dancing was over: enough to leave space for the remainder to walk about in some comfort: and now was the time for a heroine, who had not yet played a very distinguished part in the events of the evening, to be noticed and admired. Every five minutes, by removing some of the crowd, gave greater openings for her charms. She was now seen by many young men who had not been near her before. Not one, however, stared with rapturous wonder on beholding her, no whisper of eager inquiry ran round the room, nor was she once called a divinity by anybody. Yet Catherine was in very good looks, and, had the company only seen her three years before, they would *now* have thought her exceedingly handsome.

She *was* looked at, however, and with some admiration; for, in her own hearing, two gentlemen pronounced her to be a pretty girl. Such words had their due effect: she immediately thought the evening pleasanter than she had found it before; her humble vanity was contented; she felt more obliged to the two young men for this simple praise, than a true quality heroine would have been for fifteen sonnets in celebration of her charms, and went to her chair in good humour

with everybody, and perfectly satisfied with her share
of public attention.

To the Rector at seventy, Bath might not have been so
marvelous as to Catherine at seventeen, but he found it a
cheerful place to which to retire. So did the family. They
would not be strangers; relatives and friends of theirs were
there in good society. The house at No. 4 Sidney Place was
neither too large for comfort nor too small for dignity, and
it looked out on gardens. When they moved to Twenty-
Seven Green Park Buildings there still were trees. Enough
of the old furniture went with them to make the new feel at
home; Jane reported that "the two little tables have arrived;
they are both covered with green baize and send their best
love." Bath weather was mild enough for one to stay there
through the year—if he had a stout umbrella—and when
they took those trips to the seaside it would be purely for
pleasure.

Jane found more of that in Lyme Regis than elsewhere. They had a little house near the sea and not too far from the Assembly Rooms for them to walk back from a party, a manservant going before with a lantern. The landscape at Lyme is so lovely that when Jane went home she took it with her—the main street hurrying down to the sea, the curve of the cliffs to the east, the little bay at Charmouth from whose low rocks she watched the tide while the people she had brought with her unseen went on living in her mind, taking on lives of their own as they had begun to do in Steventon when her novels started to take shape, as they now were doing while her eyes were on the ebb and flow. She walked on the Cobb, that rugged old breakwater that made so popular a promenade. There was a place, she thought, where something dramatic might take place in a novel—as in time it did. It had been on the Cobb, they told her, that Monmouth had landed on his ill-fated Rebellion against King James—but when the next generation told that to Tennyson he said, "Don't talk to me of the Duke of Monmouth.

Show me the exact spot where Louisa Musgrove fell!" And as long as anyone reads a novel in English, people will take *Persuasion* with them to the Cobb and try to find the steps down which the impetuous Louisa insisted upon being "jumped"—and find instead an inscription saying that in the meantime that part of the Cobb has been rebuilt.

The Rector still enjoyed life, but less of it was left to him than he realized. In the fifth year of his retirement a day came when he was not feeling so well. On the next he went to sleep smiling, and though he did not wake, the smile remained. It was there while Jane was writing to Captain Frank in the squadron blockading Napoleon, "His tenderness as a Father, who can do justice to?"

Now there would not be six hundred a year for the women of the family to live on, and they went into lodgings while the brothers went into action. With the family blend of affection and good sense, each one guaranteed what he could send his mother regularly, according to his income and his obligations. Mrs. Austen wrote from a full heart that, though one hundred and fifty pounds a year was the whole of her own income, "my good sons had done all the rest." Those who had most gave most, those who had less, not so much, but she knew that each one gave gladly. The dangers of invasion were only just over when the Austens, with Martha Lloyd, joined Captain Frank and his bride at Castle Square, Southampton.

Chapter Sixteen

CASTLE SQUARE inherited its name from the Norman castle inside the corner of medieval Southampton's city wall. In the course of centuries it had crumbled and the space was cleared for houses with gardens, but where the Norman keep had stood, an eccentric nobleman had built a sort of castle of his own. For lack of space it had to be small, but it had castellations and battlements and whatever the Marquis thought it should have, and as he was constantly thinking of something else to do to it, it already blocked the Austens' view on one side with something on which a fastidious eye could not care to dwell. The eyes of a young nephew, however, were charmed by something he could watch from his window on a visit, looking down into the little courtyard next door on a fine day. A light carriage would be drawn out and six tiny ponies, sometimes eight, harnessed to it in pairs, the littlest and lightest-colored in the lead. Then the boys who managed them would take their places, and the Marchioness—a large, wide woman— would take her seat and jingle away on her progress through the town. It was like a scene from a toy theater.

The view from the other side was more congenial to Jane. The ancient city wall was the boundary of their present garden. Leaning upon it, she looked out over the sea—much nearer then than now to the foot of the great wall—as from the low rocks at Lyme Regis she had watched the tide go out and come in.

The friendliest of us may come to a period when we feel that we have friends enough; the period passes, but while it lasts we do not enlarge our acquaintance. This was such a time. The Austens had more invitations than they knew what to do with, but this place was for them no continuing city. Jane and Martha attended two of the Southampton Assemblies held in winter in the Long Room of the Dolphin Inn, and found one of these rather more amusing than they had expected; at least Jane, arriving past nine and leaving before twelve, did not yawn till the last quarter of an hour. "It was the same room in which we danced fifteen years ago!" she wrote. "I thought it all over—and in spite of the shame of being so much older, felt with thankfulness that I was quite as happy now as then." It went to her heart to see so many young women standing by without partners. She knew what she would have felt at their age if a woman of thirty-three had taken away a partner, and though somewhat to her surprise she was asked to dance, she gratefully declined and watched proceedings from the raised seats.

The Long Room was the north end of what is now the dining room of the lovely Dolphin Inn—still lovely, for the furious blitz that swept Southampton stopped short at the very edge of the Dolphin. Lunching there on a busy day, it takes very little imagination to see in one's mind's eye the same well-proportioned room differently lighted, filled with gentlemen and ladies differently dressed, and among them a still slender figure with a touch of sadness in her bright eyes, not for herself but because these young girls to whom the ball belonged were not getting the happiness they had every right to expect!

But in general the Austens did their best to dodge invitations now. Everything for them was temporary. Where they were going was not yet quite settled, but they were not going to stay here. Edward wanted his mother and sisters nearer his own family in some suitable house on one of his own estates. There was one in the neighborhood of Godmersham, near Canterbury, and one near Chawton Manor in Hampshire; they might have either house. There had been enough of this moving about. Next time they settled it would be to stay.

Cassandra and Jane, changing places, were exchanging notes on nieces. Cassandra at Castle Square was entertaining Anna, now fifteen; it was safe to expect from her anything unexpected, such as having her hair cut off short because that was the fashion, regardless of how it made her look. Indeed, "an Anna with variations, but she cannot have reached her last for that is always the most nourishing and showy; she is at about her third or fourth, which are usually simple and pretty"—thus Miss J. Austen, who played the piano.

Jane at Godmersham was finding that Edward's Fanny, just Anna's age, was likely to be to her almost another sister. "I did not think," she owned, "that a niece would ever have been so much to me." It was a wonderful visit. Elizabeth, Edward's beautiful wife, was expecting another baby, but they came so regularly this fitted smoothly into her gentle management of the great establishment and the great number of servants required to run it. Jane fitted without effort into this wealthy ease, but if Cassandra's letters left out details of housekeeping at Southampton, she demanded them. "My present elegances have not made me different in such matters," she wrote. "I am still a Cat when I see a Mouse."

Everything so revolved around Elizabeth Austen at Godmersham, everyone so loved and needed her, that no one dreamed she could die. But she did. After Jane's beautiful visit had ended and just before Cassandra's had begun, the baby was born. In fifteen years Elizabeth Austen had brought eleven children into this world. The last one sent her out of it.

Fanny, not yet sixteen, must now become the mainspring of the house, the comfort of her father; she must prove her love for her mother by taking her place with the children. Edward, dazed with grief, yet with "a disposition that will gradually lead him to comfort," needed now more than ever to have his mother and sisters within reach. There was a house at Chawton, just across the park from the Manor House. It was called a cottage, but it was large enough for three families to be living in it when first I went to Chawton. It was on the quiet village street, standing where the road to Winchester branches from the Gosport road, near enough to the Manor House and just far enough from it for the Austens to be by themselves when they needed to be. To all three, but to Jane the most, even before they had seen the cottage, it was home.

Edward set men at work at once to fit it for them. There were two good-sized parlors, one at either side of the front door that opened directly on the road at the spot where two roads met. The large window in the larger parlor gave those inside a fine view of post chaises passing on both roads, but as it also gave the post chaises a fine view of the interior, it was bricked up and the room made to look out into the garden at the side. The re-stocking of this garden, an old-fashioned one, could be left for the newcomers themselves, but the house, inside and out, would be ready by the time they were.

One thing more remained to do before they left Southampton. Jane made one effort to get back that manuscript "by a Lady" from the publisher who had not published it. Not to reveal who had written it, she sent him a note with a return address to "Mrs. Ashton Dennis, Post Office, Southampton," Politely reminding him that he had already kept it six years and that, unless he replied, "I shall feel myself at liberty to procure the publication of my work by applying elsewhere." That sounds as if Henry, who talked brilliantly but whose writings never used a short word when a long would do, had a hand in this letter. But when the publisher did reply, saying sharply that if the author or anybody acting for her tried to publish that book anywhere else, he would "take proceedings to stop the sale," Mrs. Ashton Dennis went back into nothingness and the book had still more time to wait. No matter. Other books were crowding to come out, and here would be the place from which they would come; crowding to be written, and here would be the place to write them. The long interval of checks and disappointments, of revising and re-casting, was at an end. The full tide of energy and inspiration was flowing. From now on it would flow free.

Chapter Seventeen

CHAWTON COTTAGE meant to Jane—never one to wait for enjoyment until there was an occasion for it—that now enjoyment and occasion had come together. Even moving in was merriment. New arrangements were planned for happiness. She would have a new piano, the best to be got for thirty guineas, and practice country dances so that nieces and nephews who came to visit—and wherever she was they always came to visit Aunt Jane—should always have music at their disposal for dancing.

The Rector at Chawton had a younger brother unmarried, Mr. Papillon, and old Mrs. Knight told Cassandra it might be a good thing for Jane to marry him. She wrote back, "I am much obliged to Mrs. Knight for such a proof of the interest she takes in me, and she may depend upon it that I *will* marry Mr. Papillon, whatever may be his reluctance or my own." The old garden was in a garden's most alluring and satisfactory state—it was *going* to be beautiful. "You cannot imagine, it is not in human nature to imagine what a nice walk we have round the orchard. I hear that an apricot has been detected on one of the trees." Jane must have syringas and a laburnum: had not her favorite poet written about

.... Laburnum, rich
In streaming gold; syringas, iv'ry pale ...

And if Cowper loved them, why should they not be there? There must be peonies, too, and mignonette and heartsease, and would not a sapling, set out in front, grow to make a shady tree beside the window? There would be time for it to grow. They were here to stay.

Mrs. Austen, too, had a new lease of life that took her into the garden, but on the vegetable side. As practical at seventy as she had been as a bride and just as unconcerned with what the neighbors might think about what she wore, she put on a workman's green blouse and dug potatoes. The housekeeping was turned over to her daughters; Jane made breakfast at nine and kept track of tea and sugar; the rest was Cassandra's and when she was at Godmersham Jane and the maids carried on. The new piano was in the larger parlor, the smaller was the sitting room for everybody. Upstairs were six bedrooms, downstairs the usual rooms where meals were prepared and served, and nowhere in the house a separate writing room for Jane. That made no difference. She had never had a study of her own, and since they left Steventon there had been no room where she could sit by herself and write. Now, after all this moving about from one house to another, Jane could come to rest once more in the family sitting room, with the current of family life moving round her, and write to her heart's content. Anyone passing by on the street could see her through the window, seated at her little mahogany box-desk, but coming in meant going through the door and when Jane found that this door creaked, she would not let it be mended. When she heard that particular squeak she knew she would have just time enough to slip under the blotting-paper the little sheets on which she was writing and rise to greet the visitor.

When the visitors were young cousins, they did not know that Aunt Jane had been writing a novel when they rushed in, and that when they had rushed out, their news welcomed with affectionate interest, out would come the hidden paper and its conversation go on from the very point at which it had left off. There was no stopping the process of creation now going on. More than one novel now was ready to go to a publisher, and the one Jane chose to go first had begun in Steventon as *Elinor and Marianne*.

About all that now remained of it was the sort of girls these two were and their names. On the title page was *Sense and Sensibility: a novel in three volumes. By a Lady. London: Printed for the author, by C. Roworth, Bell-Yard, Temple-bar, and published by T. Egerton, Whitehall, 1811.*

This showed that the author believed in it enough to stand the expense of having it published. It was the last time she had to do so. Jane went to London more than once and stayed with Henry and Eliza while the proofs of her book were coming from the press. Eliza was as much at home in London society as she had been in France, and even more fond of Jane than she had been at first sight. Henry was so proud of his sister and so delighted with the book that he could hardly keep from telling everyone who wrote it.

They took Jane to the theater, went shopping with her for bonnets, colored muslin at three-and-six a yard and silk stockings—a bargain at twelve shillings a pair—and wound up with an evening party on the grand scale, eighty persons invited, professional singers and a famous harp player, flowers under every mirror and the house not clear till after twelve. High time it was, too; Jane could not quite depend on Charles's ship being in the Channel because the Captain who told her so at the party was certainly "in liquor"—not intoxicated, of course, but headed that way.

With all this, Cassandra feared that Jane might be too busy to think of *Sense and Sensibility*. No indeed, she was "never too busy to think of S. and S. I can no more forget it than a mother can forget her sucking child. I have had two sheets to correct but the last one only brings us to W's first appearance." And Henry was hurrying the printer. Old Mrs. Knight could hardly wait for the book to come out: it would have been harder for her had she known what Willoughby's first appearance would bring about. The year was then in May, peonies were out at Chawton and the borders would

soon be bright with pinks and sweet williams, but it was
November before the book appeared, promptly sold out its
first edition, started toward the second, and set people who
kept up with new novels saying, "Have you read *Sense and
Sensibility?*"

At this distance one may wonder why it made this stir on
first appearance. A person to whom a new novel is recommended usually asks what it is "about," and to say in a few
words what this one is about makes it sound quite like a
number of other novels. To spread as it did from reader to
reader without any advertising, that first year, they must
have found something about it that was quite different. In
a few words, it is about two sisters, Elinor and Marianne
Dashwood, not in the least like Jane and Cassandra except
in their love for each other and that they lived at the Austens' social level. Both Dashwood sisters had good looks
and one had real beauty; each fell in love and was loved in
return; each thought herself engaged or on the verge of it,
and found that the object of her affections was engaged to
someone else; both suffered and were happily married before
the last page, one to somebody else. One was not all "sense"
and the other all "sensibility"; each had some of both qualities and what made the story was that the proportions so
differed. Marianne had such vivid emotions, such romantic
enthusiasms and rejections, that her common sense at crises
was all but swept away till rescued by her generous heart.
Elinor, not much older, brought good sense to bear on her
own emotional shocks—indeed, on her general view of
life—but it was as much her sensitive awareness of what
her mother and sister would suffer if they knew what she
was suffering, that kept her silent to bear it alone. It was
her own sensibility that made her understand the grief her

sister was undergoing with more clamor.

Willoughby's coming on the scene, early in the story, brings out the contrasts in the two sisters and the affection that reconciles them. His dramatic entrance has been followed by his first morning call; Marianne finds that they have the same love for dancing and for music, delight in the same books, and have in general the same eagerness and enthusiasm. After he has gone, Elinor laughingly comments on the extent of ground they have covered:

> "Well, Marianne," said Elinor, as soon as he had left them, "for *one* morning I think you have done pretty well. You have already ascertained Mr. Willoughby's opinion in almost every matter of importance. You know what he thinks of Cowper and Scott; you are certain of his estimating their beauties as he ought, and you have received every assurance of his admiring Pope no more than is proper. But how is your acquaintance to be long supported, under such extraordinary dispatch of every subject of discourse! You will soon have exhausted each favorite topic. Another meeting will suffice to explain his sentiments on picturesque beauty and second marriages, and then you can have nothing further to ask."

> "Elinor," cried Marianne, "is this fair? is this just? are my ideas so scanty? But I see what you mean. I have been too much at my ease, too happy, too frank. I have erred against every commonplace notion of decorum! I have been open and sincere when I ought to have been reserved, spiritless, dull, and deceitful: —had I talked only of the weather and the roads, and had I spoken only once in ten minutes this reproach would

have been spared."

"My love," said her mother. "You must not be offended with Elinor—she was only in jest. I should scold her myself, if she were capable of wishing to check the delight of your conversation with our new friend." Marianne was softened in a moment.

In short, one sister did not stand for Sense and the other for Sensibility, but when the story is read for the first time it might sound that way—and at that period it was no disadvantage to a book to sound that way. It would be, now. The first novel that Jane Austen published is by no means the one most likely to start a young person off on a lifelong experience with her books. My own copies of all six of her novels have been for years in a state of advanced dilapidation ; the only one whose covers have not yet collapsed is *Sense and Sensibility*, because steady wear and tear on it did not set in till I was myself far enough from actually being young to appreciate a young girl's capacity for intensity of feeling and the genius that could so create it in the character of Marianne. In conventional romances turned out at that time, a lovely young girl so recklessly trustful would have met the conventional fate; Marianne does not "come to grief," but the tearing grief that comes to her when her dream ends takes possession of her as completely as did the rapture with which it began. She does not "stoop to folly"; her foolishness is on a high level. But no calculated frenzy, no studied speech, could reach the height of those silent moments when Elinor, wakened by stifled sobs in the icy dawn of a January day, sees "Marianne, only half-dressed ... kneeling against one of the window seats for the sake of all the little light she could command from it, and writing as fast as a continual flow of tears would permit her"—writing for the last time to Willoughby.

Novel readers of the year found themselves by the time they came to the last page of the book, personally and intimately acquainted with everybody in it and very glad they were—and wondering, perhaps, how this had been brought about by the unknown author. She had said so few words about these people—but there they were, to the life. More than that. They were living. People rather wished this Lady would give them something more to read.

Chapter Eighteen

JANE AUSTEN'S readers had not long to wait. Before the next year had more than begun, Jane reported, "I have my own darling child from London."

The first set of *Pride and Prejudice: A Novel. In three volumes by the author of Sense and Sensibility"* had just arrived from the same publisher.

That night a neighbor dined with the Austens. In the evening—taking care to tell her beforehand that this was a book they had heard was coming out and had asked Henry to send them when it did—they read her half the first volume. She had no idea that she was listening to the author. Jane, keeping down her pride with difficulty, said that "she really does seem to admire Elizabeth"—and then, letting out her own feelings with a rush, "I must confess that I think her as delightful a creature as ever appeared in print, and how I shall be able to tolerate those who do not like *her* at least, I do not know."

When Fanny praised the book, that to Jane was praise indeed. Her expectation of Fanny's approval had been "tolerably strong, but nothing like a certainty"; now her liking Darcy and Elizabeth would be enough, and "she might hate all the others if she would." Of course she did not. Neither did anyone else in the novel's rapidly spreading audience, not one of whom knew who wrote it—and if by any means the author could keep them from knowing, they would not.

But how could she hope to keep in a secret that Henry was so eager to let out? Jane took alarm just from hearing that someone wanted to be introduced to her. Why should they? "If I *am* a Wild Beast, I cannot help it. It is not my own fault." The secret was seeping into society; soon came the explosion. "Henry heard P. and P. warmly praised in Scotland by Lady Robert Kerr and another lady—and what does he do in the warmth of his brotherly vanity and love, but immediately tell them who wrote it! A thing once set going in that way—one knows how it spreads!—and he, dear creature, has set it going so much more than once!" It was all done from affection, she knew, but she could not help feeling that James, who had kept so still that his own son had read the novel without an idea his own aunt had written it, had shown a better sort of kindness.

In the meantime, Jane went with Henry to an exhibition of paintings in London, and Fanny would be glad to know that she could find there a portrait of Mrs. Bingley "exactly herself, size, shaped face, features and sweetness; there never was a greater likeness. She is dressed in a white gown, with green ornaments, which convinces me of what I had always supposed, that green was a favorite color with her. I dare say Mrs. D. will be in yellow." But neither there nor in two other exhibitions, though Jane looked, was there anything like Elizabeth Darcy, *née* Bennet. "I can imagine that Mr. D. prizes any Picture of her too much to like it should be exposed to the public eye. —I can imagine he would have that sort of feeling—that mixture of Love, Pride

and Delicacy."

For the people in this blessed book did not come to life on the first page and dissolve on the last. They were alive before Chapter One, and they went on living after the book left them, and Jane knew very well what they were doing, before and after. She knew what Mr. Collins was like in his clumsy schooldays, long before he made his pompous, peerless proposal to Elizabeth, and where he had picked up, on the way toward the patronage of Lady Catherine de Bourgh, that "mixture of pride and obsequiousness, self-importance and humility" that makes him so great a comic character. I am convinced that she knew what Lady Catherine de Bourgh looked like in her perambulator, though she spares us that grim sight. We know from the novels who became the husbands of Elizabeth Bennet and her elder sister Jane, and under what debatable circumstances the bouncing Lydia picked up hers, but only the Austens knew that of the other daughters Kitty married a clergyman near Pemberley while Mary had to put up with one of her uncle's clerks. That is not in the book, but the family had inside information. They asked Jane and she told them.

All these people and others, contribute to carry out the main concern of the story—to bring a gentleman who looks at a lady with indifference and a lady who looks at him with aversion, to a point where they are convinced—with good reason, mind you—that it would be the most wonderful thing in the world to marry each other. Their first meeting was certainly unpropitious. Tall, dark, handsome, unmarried and rumored to have a tremendous fortune, Darcy might be expected not only to be popular at first sight but to stay so. But a gentleman who goes to a ball and dances only with his own party, who makes it clear that he does not care to be introduced to anyone, need not expect that popularity to last. In record time he is put down as the proudest man in the world, one who thinks himself above his company.

As a matter of fact, he is. His ancestry impressive, his family distinguished, he inherited great wealth and fine estates and had taken on fastidious tastes—and nobody had laughed at him yet, in all his life. Elizabeth Bennet could laugh at herself when she overheard him say she was not handsome enough to tempt him to dance, and tell the story on herself to her friends, but she would not have been human had she admired him for it. However, as he sees more of her, his admiration of her grows, while her dislike of him increases as she hears more about him. Both these emotions are at their highest point when Darcy explodes into the world's prize proposal— "In vain have I struggled. It will not do. You must allow me to tell you how ardently I admire and love you." There is more of that scene, but you must read it for yourself.

His struggle has been so evident, the infuriating reasons he gives for it are so explicit, that Elizabeth not only will not marry him but tells him exactly why. No lightning change comes over their natures. They part in resentment. He writes her one letter—a good long one, loftily putting her right on one matter of fact on which she has been misinformed—and it takes plenty of time and a reasonable amount of unexpected experience to overcome her prejudice by opening her eyes to his character, and to open Darcy's eyes to what he must have looked like to anyone with Elizabeth's high ideas of what it was to act like a gentleman. But all the way along we are so continuously entertained, the conversation is so sparkling, the very scenery so full of sunshine that no one ever seems to read *Pride and Prejudice* once and be done with it. The usual procedure, the last word reached, is to turn back all the leaves to the first sentence and begin once more:

It is a truth universally acknowledged, that a single man in possession of a good fortune, must be in need of a wife.

Chapter Nineteen

WHEN Jane wrote to her sister, just before the first copy of *Pride and Prejudice* reached Chawton, that she had come away from a card party "leaving just as many for their round table as there were at Mrs. Grant's," this casual reference to something of which her sister would be well aware shows how steadily Jane's writing must have been going on ever since her life began again at Chawton Cottage. For what takes place at Mrs. Grant's round table does not occur till well along in *Mansfield Park*, which had been begun nearly a year before *Sense and Sensibility* came out and almost two years before *Pride and Prejudice* appeared. In all the excitements of publication and tasks of pre-publication, Jane's third novel to be published went steadily on. Now, in 1814, *Mansfield Park: a Novel in Three Volumes by the author of Sense and Sensibility and Pride and Prejudice*, her first novel begun at Chawton, went out to an audience prepared for something to enjoy.

They soon found themselves moving in elevated circles. In the very first sentence Miss Maria Ward "had the good luck to captivate Sir Thomas Bertram, of Mansfield Park, in the county of Northampton, and to be thereby raised to

the rank of a baronet's lady, with all the comforts and consequences of a handsome house and large income." Among
such comforts the greater part of the action takes place, but
as her sisters did not do so well, it has a wider range. Lady
Bertram's husband could, by making his friend, the Rev.
Mr. Norris, parson at Mansfield, start the second sister's
marriage on a good income, but little could be done for the
third sister's prospects. She married "in the common phrase,
to disoblige her family, and by fixing on a Lieutenant of Ma-
rines, without education, fortune or connections, did it very
thoroughly." Lady Bertram was easygoing enough to forget
the whole affair, including her sister's existence, but Mrs.
Norris by pointing out to Mrs. Price, at some length and
more than once, the extent of her imprudence, had brought
it about that for eleven years she had scarcely written at all,
and all that was known about her at Mansfield came through
Mrs. Norris, who liked nothing better than going about
not doing good. By that time poor Mrs. Price had learned
that the upkeep of pride is expensive. Expecting her ninth
child, she wrote to ask what might possibly be done for the
future of the others. The letter, from her heart, went to the
hearts of the Bertrams, even to that of Mrs. Norris, who
had not much of any. They responded, each in his or her
own way. "Sir Thomas sent friendly advice and professions,
Lady Bertram despatched money and baby-linen, and Mrs.
Norris wrote the letters."

So it was that from the crowded, scrambling life of a
poor family in Portsmouth, Fanny Price at ten years old
was suddenly caught up and set down permanently in the
ease, comforts and advantages of a rich one. So it is that
Edmund, second son of the house, sixteen and home from
Eton, comes upon the heroine of Miss Austen's novel, alone

upon the attic stairs, quietly crying her eyes out.

From sheer compassion he makes his way through her almost impenetrable shyness, seeks out her sorrow and starts her on its first solace—writing a letter to her adored brother William. Jane Austen knew what shyness had meant to her, even as a beloved child in a happy family; she could understand how it might cut off all help from a lonesome, heartbroken child, and with what devotion Fanny would regard the only one who broke through to come to her rescue. It is hopeless devotion that never loses hope. Through the story it feeds its own flame, glowing as gently as Fanny's own nature. For a hero and a heroine, Edmund and Fanny have the disadvantages of being thoroughly good.

These disadvantages do not weigh at all on Mary Crawford and her brother Henry. They are Worldly. Most of us feel closer to them for being so, and it must be admitted that if Miss Crawford had overcome her objections to being a clergyman's wife and given in—as she was on the point of doing—to Edmund Bertram's uncompromising courtship, she would have found life with him more moral than merry. But while a heroine may be pointed out by the author as "My Fanny," anyone may choose a favorite character at will, and Miss Crawford's attractions so far overshadow Fanny's that the greater part of the book is quite as much hers. Jane Austen herself said, before the novel was published, that it would have "a complete change of subject—ordination," which tells as much about it as if she had said it would be bound in brown. The plot does turn on whether Edmund will be a clergyman or Mary Crawford's husband, as she will not let him be both if she can possibly help it. But this plot turns more than once, the private theatricals have as much to do with Maria Bertram's fate as ordination has with Edmund's future— and if you ask people who keep on reading *Mansfield Park* what comes first to their minds when it is mentioned, nine out of ten will instantly mention the private theatricals.

Those unforgettable, unforgotten theatricals! Here they take place in the billiard room at Mansfield Park, jettisoning the billiard table and taking for a greenroom the personal apartment of Sir William, he being at the time in the West Indies. But they came straight from the barn at Steventon where the Comtesse de Feuillide was so brilliant in comedy and Henry so dashing in the lead and a little girl too young to be given a part was taking part in everything before the play and behind the scenes. Mary Crawford is not Eliza de Feuillide; Jane Austen never drew a character from a single model. Eliza, for sixteen years Henry Austen's well-beloved wife, was dying now, slowly and in pain. Just before the novel was finished her life in this world was over—but in the memory of the creator of Mary Crawford that bright creature was living who had held off Henry's courtship because she could not bring her mind to give up "dear liberty and dearer flirtation"; who might perhaps be persuaded by a few months in the country to endure a state of sober matrimony but found from a few weeks in London "how little the state suits her taste." Perhaps Miss Crawford might not have had such charm if Eliza had not shown Miss Austen how charming a Worldly Person can be. For in the conflict between material and spiritual values that goes on throughout *Mansfield Park* —and that may be why she feared it would not be "half so entertaining" as its predecessors—Miss Austen is on the other side from Miss Crawford. Without saying so, she lets you see that she is on the side of the angels.

Writing the novel—longer by a quarter than *Pride and Prejudice*—went on steadily, swiftly, surely. Jane Austen, almost at the summit of her maturer powers, was still working with "two or three families" in circumstances with which she was familiar, but over a broader field and with sharper contrasts of character, education and environment. Her sailor brothers had part in it. She wrote to Frank at sea to borrow his ships: "Shall you object to my mentioning the *Elephant* in it, and two or three of your old Ships ? I *have* done it but it shall not stay, to make you angry. They are only just mentioned—" And when Captain Francis Austen reached the Portsmouth scenes in the third volume of the new novel, there was the *Elephant*—his own ship—in the harbor. When Fanny Price's sailor-brother William comes upon the scene in the second, Jane Austen knew from her own experience how Fanny felt when she found that after so long at sea "this dear William would soon be amongst them," and found herself "watching in the hall, in the lobby, on the stairs, for the first sound of the carriage which was to bring her a brother." She knew the warmhearted, blunt fondness of a young sailor who could say of a sister's new way of doing her hair, "Do you know, I begin to like that queer fashion already, though when I first heard of such things being done in England I could not believe it … but Fanny can reconcile me to any thing." The topaz cross Charles bought for Jane out of his first prize-money went with Fanny to her first ball, changing to amber before it reached print, and much depended on the chain that went with that amber cross. It was Jane Austen's love not only for Charles, her "own particular little brother," but also for Frank, whose long deferred promotion she announced so breathlessly to Cassandra, that gave the novel its wonderful

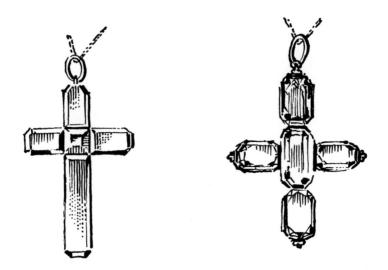

moment when William, whose promotion had come just as he had begun to think that "every body gets made but me," enters, on the point of sailing, to show his glorious new uniform to Fanny, almost sinking under what she finds in her former home:

> In this more placid state of things William re-entered, followed not far behind by his mother and Betsey. He, complete in his Lieutenant's uniform, look-ing and moving all the taller, firmer and more graceful for it, and with the happiest smile over his face, walked up directly to Fanny—who, rising from her seat, looked at him for a moment in speechless admiration, and then threw her arms round his neck to sob out her various emotions of pain and pleasure.

There is a resounding elopement with a scandal that

gets into the newspapers—and if you think the elopement too sudden, remember how much Jane Austen knew about character and what education, good or bad, can do to it, and you may see that the character and education of both parties had been leading them straight towards that catastrophe long before Henry Crawford suddenly realized that he had "indulged in the freaks of a cold-blooded vanity a little too long."

On the details of the elopement Jane Austen does not linger, preferring to make clear, in as few words as possible, what happened, why it happened just then, and how it affected the lives of others concerned, whether innocent or guilty. Jane Austen has her limits; that they are self-imposed makes them just as steadily maintained and just as necessary to bear in mind. Speaking in the first person, she makes them clear in the famous paragraph that opens the closing chapter of *Mansfield Park*:

> Let other pens dwell on guilt and misery. I quit such odious subjects as soon as I can, impatient to restore everybody, not greatly in fault themselves, to tolerable comfort, and have done with all the rest.

But before she has done with the subject of sin, you know where she stands on it. She knows sin when she sees it, and will not search out another name for it.

Jane Austen's name even yet was not on the title page of the book, but its authorship was getting to be an open secret. People were not only reading *Mansfield Park* but talking about it among themselves, which usually meant telling each other what they thought about its people.

Jane, always interested in what her readers thought about her books and especially in what they thought about this one—for it had points on which they were bound to differ —collected informal opinions of *Mansfield Park* that came to her directly or by report, wrote them down and preserved them. One came from a lady who said, perhaps for the first time, what so many of us have been saying ever since: "You fancy yourself one of the family."

But from one of Jane's own family came a letter we may well believe to have pleased her in particular. It was from Jane's nephew, James Edward.

To Miss J. Austen

{By her nephew at Winchester, who had read the earlier novels, and enjoyed them, without knowing that she was the author.)
No words can express, my dear Aunt, my surprise
Or make you conceive how I opened my eyes,
Like a pig Butcher Pile has just struck with his knife,
When I heard for the very first time in my life
That I had the honour to have a relation
Whose works were dispersed through the whole of the
   nation.
I assure you, however, I'm terribly glad;
Oh dear! just to think (and the thought drives me mad)
That dear Mrs. Jenning's good-natured strain
Was really the product of your witty brain,
That you made the Middletons, Dashwoods, and all,
And that you (not young Ferrars) found out that a ball
May be given in cottages, never so small,
And though Mr. Collins, so grateful for all,
Will Lady de Bourgh his dear Patroness call.
'Tis to your ingenuity really he owed

His living, his wife, and his humble abode.
Now if you will take your poor nephew's advice,
Your works to Sir William pray send in a trice.
If he'll undertake to some grandees to show it
By whose means at last the Prince Regent might know
    it,
For I'm sure if he did, in return for your tale,
He'd make you a countess at least, without fail,
And indeed if the Princess should lose her dear life
You might have a good chance of becoming his wife.*

* *Quoted in Jane Austen. R. Brimley Johnson 1930 p. 228.*

Chapter Twenty

NOW that all the nephews and nieces knew who was writing what they all were reading, the contagion of authorship spread among them and there was a family outbreak of works in progress. These, as a matter of course, went to Aunt Jane for constructive criticism. She read every word as it came to her, and sent back reports that also tell a good deal about herself.

In the first place, she wrote to each of the writers as one author to another—one who had been at it longer than they had—and not as teacher to pupil. James Edward, just out of Winchester, where he had tossed off that schoolboy poem of congratulation, had dashed into fiction, with which Aunt Jane was kept in touch. She heard that two chapters and a half of this work had turned up missing. That, she said, was Monstrous. "It is well that *I* have not been at Steventon lately and therefore cannot be suspected of purloining them; two strong twigs and a half towards a nest of my own, would have been something.—I do not think however that any theft of that sort would be really useful to me. What should I do with your strong, manly, spirited sketches, full of variety and glow? How could I possibly join them on to the little

bit (two inches wide) of ivory on which I work with so fine
a brush, as produces little effect after much labor?" In that
affectionate message she has not only gaily offered him a
description of her method and a definition of her art, but
given him to understand that he is entitled to a method, an
art of his own.

"Anna with variations" was engaged to be married; the
wedding would not take place for six months and she was
filling in the time by writing a novel. She knew Aunt Jane
would be eager to see it in progress, and so she was, reading
each installment aloud to her mother and Cassandra, report-
ing on their reactions as well as her own, and taking it apart
so neatly that Anna could see for herself what would be well
to change. At Chawton they were, for instance, not satisfied
with the young author's Mrs. F.'s settling as tenant and near
neighbor to such a man as Sir T. H. without having some
other inducement to go there. "A woman, going with two
girls just growing up, into a neighborhood where she knows
nobody but one man, of not very good character, is an awk-
wardness which so prudent a woman as Mrs. F. would not
be likely to fall into. Remember, she is very prudent;—you
must not let her act inconsistently. Give her a friend, and
let that friend be invited to meet her at the Priory, and we
shall have no objection to her dining there as she does; but
otherwise, a woman in her situation would hardly go there,
before she had been visited by other families."

Notice that Jane Austen does not call the attention of
young Anna—who had evidently been reading *Sense and
Sensibility*—to the deft manner in which that work pre-
pares the ground in advance for Mrs. Dashwood to bring
her daughters, just growing up, into a new neighborhood
where she knows but one family. Notice also that with

no more than a comma and a dash the letter goes on: "I like the scene itself, the Miss Lesleys, Lady Anne and the Music, very much," and that throughout, when she points out anything in Anna's story that needs change, she mentions something else too good to be touched.

As usual in these letters to beginners whom she loves, Jane Austen gives Anna, as one author to another, an insight into her own methods: "You are now collecting your people delightfully, getting them exactly into such a spot as is the delight of my life; three or four families in a country village is the very thing to work on—and I hope you will write a great deal more, and make full use of them while they are so very favorably arranged." Also, Anna is on no account to let her Devereux Forester "plunge into a 'vortex of dissipation.' I do not object to the Thing, but I cannot bear the expression; it is such thorough novel slang—and so old, that I dare say Adam met with it in the first novel he opened."

Anna's hero had found her Cecilia more interesting because he had been in love with her Aunt; Jane pounced on that with glee. "I like the idea: a very proper compliment to an Aunt!—I rather imagine indeed that neices (sic) are seldom chosen but in compliment to some Aunt or other. I dare say Ben was in love with me once, and would never have thought of *you* if he had not supposed me dead of scarlet fever."

The book was not yet finished when Anna Austen married Ben Lefroy. Simple weddings were just now the right thing among the right people; social climbers had been making too many lace veils, too much white satin and general flamboyance unpopular with those who did not need to climb. Anna, in white muslin with an embroidered silk shawl the color of spring sunlight and on her head a lace-trimmed cap, went early in the morning with her parents and two little bridesmaids in white bonnets, all together in the family carriage to meet Ben Lefroy in the old church at Steventon. Her father gave her away, his father married them, and the two families came back to the usual substantial family breakfast—with the added touch of chocolate and a wedding cake. Anna's novel went on a little longer and gradually faded away. One day, one of her children watched her burn the manuscript in the grate. It made a fine blaze as one after another the pages fed the flame. When the child was old enough to know what was written on those pages, she asked her mother why she had burned them —and Anna told her she could not bear to look them over without Aunt Jane.

Fanny had another sort of problem. Trying to make up her own mind on a matter concerning her whole life's happiness and not quite sure what her own mind was, she laid the matter before the perfect confidante. Aunt Jane, so close to her in mind and heart, might understand her better than she did herself. When they had been together in London, Aunt Jane had thought Fanny really in love with one of her suitors, and had been glad he seemed so suitable. Well, Fanny *had* been in love with him. She had encouraged a good young man to hope—as much as a decorous young lady might—and now that she was practically sure of him and he probably thought he was sure of her, to her dismay Fanny found that she was not so much in love. She was not interested in anyone else, but her interest in him was cooling off. Should she try—indeed, she had been trying—to revive it again? What should she do? All this was so confidential that her father brought the letter inside a roll of music; Aunt Jane, who usually read letters from Fanny to the family as soon as they arrived, was not to let even dear Aunt Cassandra know that this one had arrived at all. "Your dear Papa most conscientiously hunted about till he found me alone in the dining parlor; your Aunt had seen that he had a parcel to deliver. As it was, however, I do not think any thing was suspected."

As for advice, what Aunt Jane substituted for it was just

what Fanny needed; she went into the same flutter as Fanny's but kept her head. "My dear Fanny, I am writing what will not be of the smallest use to you. I am feeling differently every moment, and shall not be able to suggest a single thing that can assist your mind. I could lament in one sentence and laugh in the next, but as to opinion or counsel I am sure none will be extracted worth having from this letter." She is full of interest and concern; poor dear Mr. J. P.! "Oh! dear Fanny, your mistake has been one that thousands of women fall into. He was the *first* young man who attached himself to you. That was the charm, and most powerful it is." His abilities, education, situation in life, character, are all they should be, "and he is I dare say such a scholar as your agreeable idle brothers would ill bear comparison with." In fact, the more she writes about him the warmer grow her feelings and the more she inclines toward thinking it might be a good idea for Fanny to fall in love with him again. Perhaps he *may* not be quite perfect. "There *are* such beings in the world, perhaps one in a thousand, as the Creature you and I should think perfection ... but such a person may not come in your way, or if he does, he may not be the oldest son of a man of fortune, the brother of your particular friend, and belonging to your own county. Think of this, Fanny." (Well she knew Fanny was thinking of it!) His only fault seems to be modesty and that will wear off; "he will catch your ways if he belongs to you." Her brothers shine more, but "wisdom is better than wit and in the long run will certainly have the laugh on her side; and don't be frightened by the idea of his acting more strictly up to the precepts of the New Testament than others. —And now, my dear Fanny, having written so much on one side of the question, I shall turn round and entreat you not to commit yourself farther, and not to think of accepting him unless you really do like him. Anything is to be preferred or endured rather than marrying without affection; and if his deficiencies of manner etc. etc. strike you more than all his good qualities, if you continue to think strongly of them, give him up at once. ... I have no doubt of his suffering a good deal for a time, a great deal, when he finds that he must give you up, but it is no creed of mine, as you must be well aware, that such sort of disappointments kill anybody."

This was by no means the only gentleman to find Fanny Knight charming. That she truly must have been appears from the effect of her cumulative confidences on Aunt Jane. "My dearest Fanny, you are inimitable, irresistible. You are the delight of my life. Such letters, such entertaining letters as you have lately sent! Such a description of your queer little heart! ... You are the paragon of all that is silly and sensible, commonplace and eccentric, sad and lively, provoking and interesting— You are so odd!—and all the time, so perfectly natural—so peculiar in yourself, and yet so like every body else! It is very, very gratifying to me to know you so intimately. You can hardly think what a pleasure it is to me, to have such thorough pictures of your heart."

On the wall of Chawton Cottage hangs today a portrait, to the life, of Fanny Knight when as Lady Knatchbull she was as well married as Jane could have wished. There, in the matron, are the intent dark eyes, the aristocratic nose, the "live" look in every feature, of the girl whose contradictions Jane Austen found so fascinating.

About that time we may thank another correspondent not so sparkling for bringing out another bit of light on how Jane Austen wrote. Henry fell seriously ill in London and Jane, who came in all haste to nurse him through, was generally in the sickroom, working or writing, for another novel was in hand. Here she met his physicians; Henry was important enough to have, as one of them, one of the physicians in attendance upon the Prince Regent. He told Jane that as His Royal Highness was a great admirer of her works—to the point indeed of keeping a set of them in each of the royal residences—he should be informed that Miss Austen herself was in town. Considering the Prince's career, that statement about the sets may seem surprising, but it was none the less true; one of the surprising things about this ambiguous monarch was that as a collector he had admirable taste. His librarian was instructed to call at once upon Miss Austen, express the royal appreciation, and invite her to inspect the library at Carlton House—disrespectfully but popularly known as "Nero's Palace"—where she was received by the librarian, shown around with great deference, and assured that if she should decide to dedicate any further work to the Regent, H.R.H. would consider it an honor.

Miss Austen did have a work almost ready for publication, but after she had come away, a trifle dazed because the Rev. Stanier Clarke had wrapped up his meanings in such handsome phrases, she could not be quite sure he had really meant to say that without asking for the right to do so, she could print in the book that it was "dedicated by permission" to H. R. H. The librarian made himself instantly clear on that point; it was certainly not *incumbent* upon her to dedicate anything to him, but if she should "wish to do the Regent that honor either now or at any future period," he was happy to say that she did not have to ask. And while they were on the subject of that future work, how about letting it depict the character of a clergyman (which he described in detail with one eye on the mirror) as no one seemed to have quite done justice to a clergyman in fiction, "at least of the present day"?

We have seen how politely Jane declined, as not having sufficient classical education to deal with such a character, but the Rev. Mr. Clarke, being quite without humor and filled with genuine admiration of her work, came back with the helpful suggestion that she might dedicate her next to Prince Leopold, whose marriage was impending, and that "any historical romance, illustrative of the history of the House of Cobourg, would just now be very interesting." This really was a little too much, but Jane, who knew he honestly meant to be helpful and had not a notion what nonsense he was talking, replied with perfect sincerity:

> ... I am fully sensible that an historical romance, founded on the House of Saxe Cobourg, might be much more to the purpose of profit or popularity than such pictures of domestic life in country villages as I deal in. But I could no more write a romance than an epic poem. I could not sit seriously down to write a serious romance under any other motive than to save my life; and if it were indispensable for me to keep it up and never relax into laughing at myself or at other people, I am sure I should be hung before I had finished the first chapter. No, I must keep to my own style and go on in my own way; and though I may never succeed again in that, I am convinced that I should totally fail in any other."

And there it stands, a confession of faith for which we may thank the Rev. James Stanier Clarke, who all unknowing drew it out.

Miss Austen was not much impressed by the royal permission. The chief use she made of it was to hurry the printers, who were holding up the appearance of her new book by being more than a month behind time. She wrote to her publisher—this time it was the great John Murray—to ask if there were any hope of their being quickened, and as a sort of last resort, added: "Is it likely that the printers will be influenced to greater dispatch and punctuality by knowing that the work is to be dedicated to the Prince Regent? If you can make that circumstance operate I shall be very glad." Perhaps it did; at any rate, in December of the same year *Emma; a Novel. In three volumes. By the Author of Pride and Prejudice &c. &c.* came out with an inscription in the customary form: *To His Royal Highness THE PRINCE REGENT this work is, by his Royal Highness's Permission, most respectfully dedicated, by his Royal Highness's Dutiful and Obedient Humble Servant, THE AUTHOR.*

And that is how the First Gentleman of Europe went into history as the only Royal Personage to whom Jane Austen dedicated a novel.

Chapter Twenty-one

THE comedy loses no time in starting. The first sentence of *Emma* rises from the page with the direct lift of a helicopter.

> Emma Woodhouse, handsome, clever and rich, with a comfortable home and happy disposition, seemed to unite some of the best blessings of existence; and had lived nearly twenty-one years in the world with very little to distress or vex her.

With this slightly ominous overture, the curtain rises on Hartfield, the comfortable home in which much of the action takes place, disclosing Emma Woodhouse at the moment when it comes over her with full force that unbroken bliss cannot keep up indefinitely. A wedding has just been celebrated, a happy bride departed, the guests dispersed, and Emma is left with the mixed feelings usually reserved on such occasions for the Mother of the Bride. With every reason to be glad, trying not to admit what reason she has for being sorry, she has lost "one to whom she could speak every thought as it arose, and who had such an affection for her as could never find fault."

Sixteen years before, Miss Taylor had come to Hartfield as governess to two motherless girls; Emma, the younger, was five years old. Their loss brought out all her tenderness, and by the time she had nursed Emma through the measles her life was centered in the family. When Isabella married, Miss Taylor was there to stand by Emma through the process of growing-up; "on an equal footing and with perfect unreserve," she had been such a friend as Emma could hardly hope to find again. For as a close companion she had just lost Miss Taylor. Mr. Weston, a well-to-do widower of long standing, with everyone's goodwill and goodwill towards everyone, fell in love with Miss Taylor and had this day carried her off to a home of her own and a husband who appreciated her as much as Hartfield had done.

Nothing like the last seven years was likely to happen again, Emma knew, at least in companionship of minds. From her adoring father she could not count on much of it; everyone loved the kind old gentleman, but not for his intellectual powers. Even his daughter, who loved him devotedly and fitted her life round her arrangements for his comfort, could not expect much stimulus from his conversation, nor from that of the comfortable old ladies who came in the evening for cards by his fireside. Gentle Mr. Woodhouse, who hated nothing else, hated change in anything. After seven years of his elder daughter's happy marriage he was still tenderly commiserating "poor Isabella" on having to leave home, and today he was starting on "Poor Miss Taylor—what a pity it is that Mr. Weston ever thought of her!"

This was no day when his daughter could afford the luxury of low spirits. When their friend Mr. Knightley dropped in to ask how the wedding went off, she could assure him there had not been a tear. "Oh no, we all felt that we were going to be only half a mile apart, and were sure of meeting every day." ... "Dear Emma bears every thing so well," says her father. "But, Mr. Knightley, she is really very sorry to lose poor Miss Taylor, and I am sure she *will* miss her more than she thinks for." To which Emma, at that moment missing Miss Taylor so much she never expects to get over it, can only turn away her head, "divided between tears and smiles," and turn the subject to her own cause for congratulation. She had made the match. Its success encourages her to go on.

At this Mr. Knightley cannot keep his peace. Not only a man of common sense and sound judgment, he is one of the few who can see any faults in her and the only one who tells her of them. He plainly tells her now that all she made was a lucky guess, and should she really interfere further in arranging other people's lives for them, she would do more harm to herself than good to anyone else. Mr. Woodhouse, alarmed, puts in his plea: "But, my dear, pray do not make any more matches, they are silly things, and break up one's family circle grievously." "Only one more, Papa," she laughs back and there we are, headed straight into a masterpiece of comedy.

Emma's matchmaking spins the plot. Full of energy and nothing much to do with it, so sure she is right that she sees what should be there and not what is, her two friends, talking her over by themselves, have reason to agree that "there is an anxiety, a curiosity, in what one feels for Emma. I wonder what will become of her?" It keeps us personally interested. How does she look? Hear Mrs. Weston :

"Such an eye!—the true hazel eye—and so brilliant!

regular features, open countenance, with a complexion! oh! what a bloom of full health, and such a pretty height and size; such a firm and upright figure. There is health, not merely in her bloom, but in her air, her head, her glance. One hears sometimes of a child being the 'picture of health'; now Emma always gives me the idea of being the complete picture of grown-up health. She is loveliness itself. Mr. Knightley, is not she?"

The picture is particularly well-drawn because it gives not only her looks but the effect they have on Mrs. Weston—indeed on everyone who knows her. Even Mr. Knightley admits that he loves to look at her and that "considering how very handsome she is, she appears to be little occupied with it." However:

"Emma has been meaning to read more ever since she was twelve years old. I have seen a great many lists of her drawing up at various times of books that she meant to read regularly through—and very good lists they were—very well chosen, and very neatly arranged—sometimes alphabetically, and sometimes by some other rule. The list she drew up when only fourteen—I remember thinking it did her judgment so much credit, that I preserved it some time; and I dare say she may have made out a very good list now. But I have done with expecting any course of steady reading from Emma … You never could persuade her to read half so much as you wished,—You know you could not."

"I dare say," replied Mrs. Weston, smiling, "that I thought so *then;*—but since we have parted, I can never remember Emma's omitting to do anything I wished."

Something seems curiously familiar about those lists. Some of us must have made them sometime.

So, through the testimony of eye-witnesses, stands Miss Austen's heroine, equipped to get into a chain of difficulties and delusions largely of her own making—and to emerge at last, in the fond opinion of her severest critic, "faultless in spite of all her faults."

Her first campaign might have shown her she was no campaign manager. Beginning by clearing away another suitor for her protegee Harriet, she talks the little goose into loving Mr. Elton, a young clergyman so bent on being agreeable that "when he has to please ladies every feature works," finds her plans bounce back with dizzying completeness, and is left with the duty of talking Harriet out of love with him—a feat only Mr. Elton himself can perform. But it leads to the scene of pure and delicate comedy that Jane Austen might not have written had not Fanny Knight kept her so well-informed on her emotional ups-and-downs, in which Harriet brings her *most precious treasures* that have suddenly lost value, out of the tiny box lined with softest cotton that has enshrined them, and puts them on the fire in Emma's presence in token that all is over—and something else starting. Nothing in the situation seems contrived; one looks on at something taking place.

"However, now I will destroy it all; and it is my particular wish to do it in your presence, that you may see how rational I am grown. Cannot you guess what this parcel holds?" said she, with a conscious look.

"Not the least in the world. Did he ever give you anything?"

"No,—I cannot call them gifts; but they are things that I have valued very much."

She held the parcel towards her, and Emma read the words "Most precious treasures" on the top. Her curiosity was greatly excited. Harriet unfolded the parcel, and she looked on with impatience. Within abundance of silver paper was a pretty little Tunbridge-ware box, which Harriet opened: it was well lined with the softest cotton; but, excepting the cotton, Emma saw only a small piece of court-plaister.

"Now," said Harriet, "you must recollect."

"No, indeed, I do not."

"Dear me! I should not have thought it possible you could forget what passed in this very room about court-plaister, one of the very last times we ever met in it. It was but a very few days before I had my sore throat,—just before Mr. and Mrs. John Knightley came; I think the very evening. Do not you remember his cutting his finger with your new pen-knife, and your recommending court-plaister? But as you had none about you, and knew I had, you desired me to supply him; and so I took mine out, and cut him a piece; but it was a great deal too large, and he cut it smaller, and kept playing some time with what was left before he gave it back to me. And so then, in my nonsense, I could not help making a treasure of it; so I put it by, never to be used, and looked at it now and then as a great treat."

"My dearest Harriet!" cried Emma, putting her hand before her face, and jumping up, "you make me

more ashamed of myself than I can bear. Remember it? Ay, I remember it all now,—all, except your saving this relic: I knew nothing of that till this moment; but the cutting the finger, and my recommending court-plaister, and saying I had none about me—oh! my sins, my sins!—and I had plenty all the while in my pocket! One of my senseless tricks. I deserve to be under a continual blush all the rest of my life. Well," sitting down again, "go on; what else ?"

"And had you really some at hand yourself? I am sure I never suspected it, you did it so naturally."

"And so you actually put this piece of court-plaister

by for his sake," said Emma, recovering from her state of shame and feeling, divided between wonder and amusement; and secretly she added to herself: "Lord bless me! when should I ever have thought of putting by in cotton a piece of court-plaister that Frank Churchill had been pulling about! I never was equal to this."

"Here," resumed Harriet, turning to her box again, "here is something still more valuable,—I mean that has been more valuable,—because this is what did really once belong to him, which the court-plaister never did."

Emma was quite eager to see this superior treasure. It was the end of an old pencil, the part without any lead.

"This was really his," said Harriet. "Do not you re-member one morning?—no, I dare say you do not. But one morning—I forget exactly the day—but perhaps it was the Tuesday or Wednesday before that evening, he wanted to make a memorandum in his pocket-book; it was about spruce beer. Mr. Knightley had been tell-ing him something about brewing spruce beer, and he wanted to put it down; but when he took out his pencil, there was so little lead that he soon cut it all away, and it would not do, so you lent him another, and this was left upon the table as good for nothing. But I kept my eye on it; and as soon as I dared, caught it up, and never parted with it again from that moment."

"I do remember it," cried Emma; "I perfectly re-member it. Talking about spruce beer,—oh, yes! Mr. Knightley and I both saying we liked it, and Mr. Elton's seeming resolved to learn to like it too. I perfectly remember it.—Stop! Mr. Knightley was standing just here, was not he? I have an idea he was standing just here."

"Ah! I do not know. I cannot recollect. It is very odd, but I cannot recollect. Mr. Elton was sitting here, I remember, much about where I am now."

"Well, go on."

"Oh! that's all. I have nothing more to show you, or to say, except that I am now going to throw them both behind the fire, and I wish you to see me do it."

Then there is the ball at the Crown Inn with the entrance speech of Miss Bates, a *tour de force* that begins as she comes through the front door, and holds us in thrall for two pages without a break until with "Everything so good!" she is seated by the fire. Blessed Miss Bates! She never knew she was one of literature's great comic characters.

There is a picnic on Box Hill—how many who picnic there today take *Emma* along to read on the spot!—which takes place at the height of an intrigue going on under the very eye of Miss Woodhouse, too "decided and open" herself to suspect anything underhand. It has the one piece of wit for which it would be hard to forgive her had she found it possible to forgive herself—and if that seems too much penitence for so few words, how many of us whose wit has for once got the better of our kindness have lain awake asking ourselves: "How *could* I ever have said that?"

Soon as the book was out, Jane began to gather opinions of it, given, heard or overheard by relatives, neighbors and friends, as she had done with *Mansfield Park*. Cassandra liked it better than *Pride and Prejudice* and less than *Mansfield Park*: Mrs. Austen found it not so interesting as the first but more entertaining than the other. Captain Charles Austen, whose set of little volumes came just before he sailed, was more delighted with *Emma* than with his favorite *Pride and Prejudice*, and read it three times on the passage. Mr. Jeffreys of the *Edinburgh Review* had been kept up three nights by it. Everyone liked Mr. Knightley and everyone still does. To be liked as well as respected, a strong man like Mr. Knightley should have one weakness; his was Emma.

These "opinions" were in the main simply "first impressions" of people reading *Emma* for the first time, in its first year, and reacting instinctively to people in the book. They showed chiefly that many now were reading Jane Austen's books and finding in them people as alive as they were themselves. Now came a voice from the heights, not only with appreciation but with authority, in a reasoned estimate of Jane's art that was in itself a recognition that the novels had entered the main stream of English literature. Sir Walter Scott's review—unsigned, of course, but it was well enough known who wrote it—came out in the *Quarterly Review*, including *Emma* in a study of the author's development of a form of fiction that "has arisen almost in our own time, which draws the characters and incidents introduced more immediately from the current of ordinary life than was permitted by the former rules of the novel."

The author had no cause to complain of that article— though she did rather wish there had been something in it about *Mansfield Park*—but if she could have looked into Sir Walter's Journal nine years later, she would have come closer to his admiration, his reverence. For she would have found that on March 14, 1826, he had put down:

Read again for the third time at least, Miss Austen's finely written novel of *Pride and Prejudice*. That young

lady had a talent for describing the involvements and feelings and characters of ordinary life which is to me the most wonderful I ever met with. The big Bow-Wow strain I can do myself like any now going; but the exquisite touch which renders ordinary commonplace things and characters interesting from the truth of the description and the sentiment, is denied to me.

That exquisite touch brought out for him, and brings out for each succeeding generation, characters so true to life itself that they are true to life today. It is the secret of Jane Austen's perennial modernity. A woman of her own time, reproducing in her novels with delicate fidelity the conditions of life around her in the early nineteenth century, we never think of what she wrote as historical novels. Time passes, and takes away with it much that has pleased the hour, but in every hour of time there is a little moment of eternity, and on that, great art lays hold. Details change, essentials remain; Jane Austen's art held fast to essentials. She was not concerned with the House of Saxe Cobourg. We come upon her people with the delight of recognizing people we know; her novels speak to any age that speaks English.

Indeed, pure English has its part in keeping her characters abreast of the times. Because that "exquisite touch" brought out in her people their difference in breeding, in education, in taste, without relying on the use of slang or bad grammar—neither of which, you remember, she had heard at home—her novels are not "dated" as catchwords of a year "date" a novel when it is read twelve months later. Some words she uses have indeed changed their meaning since she used them, but it is one of the minor pleasures in reading Miss Austen to mark what those changes have been. In *Pride and Prejudice* the word is *candor;* a "candid opinion" has come to imply that it will probably hurt your feelings, but when Elizabeth Bennet used it for her dearest sister it was a gracious word. In *Northanger Abbey* the word is *nice*; it was then in process of changing, and Henry Tilney had a word to say about that. In *Emma* the word is *elegant,* which has lost caste until it has lost meaning in phrases such as "a simply elegant time." On the lips of Emma Woodhouse it carried a delicate, desirable distinction. Jane Fairfax was "a very elegant young woman" though she did her own hair, but resplendent Mrs. Elton came off badly at first sight. "Emma would not be in a hurry to find fault, but she suspected that there was no elegance—ease, but not elegance—she was almost sure that for a young woman, a stranger, a bride, there was too much ease. Her person was rather good; her face not unpretty; but neither feature, nor air, nor voice, nor manner, were elegant. Emma thought at least it would turn out so." And indeed, indeed it did!

Chapter Twenty-two

IN the affairs of the Austens, trouble was blowing up. This no more appears in Jane Austen's later novels or affects their spirit, than the Napoleonic Wars had influenced her earlier ones, but it was, in its way, enough of a shock to make an impression on everyone in the family. The bank at Alton failed, and brought down with it Henry's London firm, Austen, Maule and Tilson, with which it was involved, in a resounding crash.

They all lost money by it, some a great deal; Henry lost everything he had, and the chance of making any more in finance. At forty-five he was ruined; all his "dreams of affluence, nay competence" were closed. No one in the family or elsewhere blamed him, but the sheer weight of the catastrophe might have crushed someone else than Henry, and almost anyone else would have needed—and taken—some time to make a complete personal readjustment. But he was not anyone else. He was still Henry. Within the year he had not only been ordained—the examiners found him particularly good in Greek—but was hard at work as a country curate of the Church of England at Bentley near Chawton village.

Jane told young Edward that "Uncle Henry preaches eloquent sermons," and fashionable London pulpits had careers for eloquence, but for the rest of his long life Henry put his whole heart into the duties of a simple country clergyman, loved by all his parishioners, young in heart and never looking really old. As Jane had said more than once: "What a Henry!"

Considering how close was the lifelong tie between brother and sister, one would scarcely expect that in these troubled months of Henry's financial downfall Jane could have done much creative writing. But it was within these months that she began and finished the deepest and most beautiful of her novels. *Persuasion* has a pensive beauty; its depth is that of something not only a love story but a story about love.

Anne Elliot's own love story had begun and ended seven years before, when she was nineteen. A young naval officer, just made commander and on shore for half a year, handsome, spirited and determined, fell rapidly and thoroughly in love with her and she with him. His hopes were high; her beauty blossomed. Confident of his future and eager to share it with her, offering a glowing warmth of affection lacking at her home, he asked her to marry him and was accepted; their happiness transformed the present and seemed to foretell the future. Her father and sister were coldly indifferent to the engagement, caring scarcely enough to be hostile; it was an alliance not acceptable to Sir Walter Elliot and neither he nor his daughter Elizabeth would accept it; so much might be taken for granted in advance. Only one other person cared enough to advise either way. This was Lady Russell, friend of Anne's dead mother, who prized the young girl's delicate loveliness— overpowered as it had been by the frontal attack of her sister's beauty—appreciated qualities in her character unnoted at home, and regarded as a sacred duty the charge of her dear Anne's future. It was Lady Russell who persuaded Anne against the engagement. The marriage would be too precarious for the happiness either of Anne or of young Captain Wentworth. It was easier for Anne to believe that marriage might impede his career than that he might not succeed in creating a great one. They parted; Wentworth, impetuous and resentful, set himself to forget her, and had to all appearances completely succeeded.

Not so with Anne. At twenty-six, she had long known what she had from the first suspected; Lady Russell had been wrong. Wentworth's success had been rapid, steady and well-deserved; Anne's happiness would be found with no other. Her love story had passed. Nothing could revive it—but nothing could have replaced it.

Now the affairs of her father, Sir Walter Elliot, baronet—vain, extravagant and obstinate—had by this time reached a crisis. However against his will it might be, and it certainly was, to clear his debts he must rent Kellynch Hall and retire to Bath, where a good address high up on Camden Place could satisfy his sense of importance and not cost so much. Elizabeth of course would go with him; Anne disliked Bath but was not consulted; at least she would be near Lady Russell.

Meanwhile Mary, the third sister, married to young Charles Musgrove, declared: "I cannot possibly do without Anne." Elizabeth replied, "Then Anne had better stay, for nobody will want her in Bath." And for the next few weeks Anne was free to keep the peace and try to bring about some order in Uppercross Cottage, not far from her old home.

The Musgroves of Uppercross, a comfortable old-fashioned couple, would have preferred their son and heir to marry Anne—as indeed he had tried to do—but were cheerfully making the best of Mary; so were their more fashionable daughters, goodhearted, lightheaded young girls.

In this unaccustomed atmosphere of domestic goodwill, the supreme test of Anne's fortitude was approaching. The Admiral who had rented Kellynch mentioned that they were "expecting a brother of Mrs. Croft's here soon; I dare say you know him by name." Captain Frederick Wentworth, all his confident predictions fulfilled, honored, distinguished, and with twenty thousand pounds prize-money made in the war, would soon be on shore again, half a mile away.

When they met, it was clear that he had not forgiven Anne Elliot. He had loved her, no woman since had seemed to equal her, but she had failed him out of timidity and over-persuasion, and her power over him was gone forever. Now he had come on shore, prepared to marry and ready to fall in love with any pleasing young woman with strength of mind and sweetness of manner—except Anne Elliot. She was "so altered he should not have known her." Said with no thought of its reaching her, it did. It was true; she could not say the same of him. Handsomer than ever, if he were altered, it had been for the better—but she had seen the same Frederick Wentworth.

All that takes place thereafter—the frank adoration and hero-worship of both Musgrove girls and the dangerous gaiety of its object; the fateful conversation overheard in the double hedgerow; the expedition to Lyme Regis with its famous climax on the Cobb and its far-reaching consequences; Captain Benwick's rapid recovery from bereavement; the domestic peace on shore of his brother-officers of whom Anne thought wistfully: "These would have been my friends"; the reappearance of Sir Walter's heir, all that goes on in and around the life of Anne Elliot—bears on the revival of Wentworth's rejected love and the recovery of Anne's relinquished happiness. The very landscape takes on the color of her quiet thoughts—"the fresh-made path spoke the farmer, counteracting the sweets of poetic despondency and *meaning to have spring again.*" All the people in the book live their own lives, each according to his own nature. But the book, in essence, is a story about love itself.

Chapter Twenty-three

BEFORE the year was out Jane Austen had finished *Persuasion*, at the last moment re-writing the crucial chapter and canceling what now seems pallid by contrast. When the new year began she was starting a new novel, *Sanditon* we now call it; writing swiftly and steadily, creating a scene and a subject different from any she had hitherto chosen, with place and people sharply etched in a curiously modern seaside real estate development.

We have had *Sanditon* since it was printed in 1925, less a first draft than a small part of a finished novel, a glittering fragment, tantalizing because no hand but Jane's can complete it, though many have tried. Years before, she had put aside two other novels, one by one: *The Watsons*, long after, was brought to a close by another hand; *Lady Susan*, a novel in letters, she herself had hurriedly ended and put away, possibly because she found the form inadequate as she had done with *Elinor and Marianne*, but more probably, I think, because in Lady Susan herself she had created her one thoroughly wicked woman and found it quite impossible to associate with her any longer.

Jane was just passing forty now. Her step was still light

and graceful, but it was less easy to walk so fast or so far as she had loved to do. The little donkey-cart with a box-seat for bringing home bundles—"Jane's cart," which now has come back to Chawton Cottage where visitors come to see it—took her more often to the village for shopping than when she thought nothing of walking to Alton and back. It took her more often along the little lanes she loved to explore. The year wore on into winter, the roads were too heavy for light carriages and the fat little donkeys were living in luxurious idleness and forgetting their education. At Chawton they had two, "but we do not use two at once; don't imagine such excesses."

Thus Jane, writing a cozy newsletter to Alethea Bigg, dropping in a light sentence about "gaining health," and adding in a postscript that the real reason of the letter was to ask for a recipe, "but I thought it genteel not to let it appear early." *Gaining* health? There was a shiver in the sound. Jane, who was health itself, must have been ill? She was indeed recovering—slowly. Cassandra, encompassing her with tenderness, felt a faint fear at her heart, not to be acknowledged even by herself. Surely Jane would soon be quite, quite well? See how gaily she was already writing again to the nieces! Writing to them, all about their affairs that she found so fascinating, she was just as interested and amused as any young girl could wish her to be. See how she loved to have them write to her! Almost casually she let fall in a letter to Fanny Knight, that she is "considerably better" now and even recovering her looks a little, though of course she must not depend on being ever very blooming again. "Sickness is a dangerous indulgence at my time of life." It was not complaint—only a backward glance of affection for that laughing young Miss J. Austen whose rosy cheeks so

brought out the brightness of her eyes. Later in the same letter she apologizes for even that touch of regret; she had been "languid and dull" when she wrote, earlier in the day; now the lights are lit, the curtains drawn, she is feeling better, much better; the saddle for the donkey is almost ready; air and exercise are just what she wants.

To Fanny, reading the letter, two of its words must have had a deeply disquieting sound. Languid? Who had ever used that word for Aunt Jane? When had she ever used it? And when had Aunt Jane ever been dull?

No one found her so, even now. The saddle came home, neat and comfortable. There was laughter and bustling about as the little donkey drew up at the garden door and Jane mounted; they set off sedately, Cassandra walking by her side. On the right of the road as you come from

Alton toward Chawton, you will see a green lane turn off.
This is Mounter's Lane; up this they went, pausing at the
loveliest bits where they could look off and the little beast
could nibble ; then back he ambled and they came home
smiling. It would be a journey to remember—the air and
the exercise.

Anna sent old Mrs. Austen a turkey and Aunt Jane said
her mother was grieving because Anna had not kept it for
herself; "such highmindedness is almost more than she can
bear." Charles's little daughter marveled over a cryptic New
Year letter from Aunt Jane that began

> Ym raed Yssac: I hsiw uoy a yppah wen raey … ,
> and went on in the same elaborate cipher to
>   Ruoy Etanutceffa Tnua,
>   Enai Netsua.

It was not so hard to read when Cassy found that all she
had to do was to hold it to a mirror—or spell it backward.
Only Aunt Jane thought of wonderful things like that; she
could even spell words with her pretty fingers, faster than
Cassy could write; sign-language, they called it.

But Jane could now be shaken by something not so great
as the bank failure she had taken in her stride. Uncle Leigh
Perrot died; he was a very rich man with no children and
Mrs. Austen was his only sister, with whom he and his wife
had always been on affectionate terms. Yet when his will was
read Mrs. Austen's name was not so much as mentioned ;
the money was left to Aunt Perrot; such of Mrs. Austen's
children as should outlive Aunt Perrot were then to have
legacies, James a large one, the others each a smaller sum.
Mrs. Austen understood why she had been left out; she had

been an invalid for so many years it had not occurred to her brother that she might outlive him. Mrs. Austen said so, like a lady, and whatever else she may have felt about the rest of the document she was too much of a lady to say. It was the sort of bequest that might have been expected from a loving husband whose wife meant to hold the power of the purse strings to the last possible moment. At any rate, it was a situation to which Jane was not accustomed: these Austens just did not have situations like that; it brought on a relapse.

"I am the only one of the legatees who has been so silly," she wrote apologetically to Charles, "but a weak body must excuse weak nerves." She told him she was living upstairs now and being petted—and by the way, if she should be needed, a hackney chariot must be sent all the way for her, as she isn't strong enough to travel any other way—and be sure that it is a green one!

This attack had been severe. Jane's chief concern had been that there should be no sittings-up with her to wear out anyone else. Her head was clear, she said; there was scarcely any pain, just feverish nights, restlessness and languor—as she told it. As they saw it, their care and tenderness redoubled.

"How to do justice to the tenderness of all my family during this illness is quite beyond me," she wrote. "Every dear brother so affectionate and so anxious! As for my Sister, words must fail me in any attempt to describe what a nurse she has been to me! ... In short, if I live to be an old woman I must expect to wish I had died now, blessed in the tenderness of such a family, and before I had survived either them or their affection." She was beginning to recover—and Cassandra was beginning to breathe again— but not easily.

The light of her life, which had sunk so low, was coming up again—slowly—too slowly. Could it be, they scarcely dared ask themselves at Chawton Cottage, that Jane was not really recovering?

The apothecary at Alton could not pretend to cope with this illness—to this day no one can be quite sure what it was—but at Winchester, sixteen miles away, on the road that went past the cottage, was a hospital with excellent physicians, one of whom came to attend Jane. At Winchester she could have the benefit of further treatment; a few weeks in that fair cathedral city, in pleasant lodgings on College Street, not far from the hospital, would bring her back to health. It would be an easy journey in the comfortable family carriage which James was sending from Steventon, and Jane was now "really a very genteel, portable sort of an invalid."

Anna Lefroy, brightly smiling but with cold fear at her heart, brought her younger sister Caroline to wish Aunt Jane a happy journey. Caroline had thought to find her in bed, but she came to meet them at the top of the steep, narrow stairs, wearing a soft dressing gown, welcoming them with the same heartfelt affection. Here was a chair by the fire for the married lady, she said, and here was a little stool for Caroline; there they sat together, talking happily till Aunt Cassy came to make sure that her patient should not be tired, and shepherded the visitors down the narrow stairs. On the wall of the bedroom, just over where they were sitting round the fire, hangs today a copy of young Caroline's recollection of that quarter-hour, written on a fair white parchment, ending simply, "and I never saw Aunt Jane again."

Cassandra and Jane were to travel light, as they had so often done on carriage-visits. Their preparations were soon made. But this time, before Jane set off for Winchester, she made her will. It was short and simple, a message of love and confidence; everything to "my dearest sister Cassandra Elizabeth" except fifty pounds to Henry and fifty to a French servant who had lost by Henry's financial crash. Cassandra would attend to any business matters; Henry, she knew, would look after her writings as if they were his own. There was nothing now to trouble her; to Winchester she could go in peace, without possessions.

It was in May that the carriage set out. The peonies, the pinks, the syringa were coming into bloom in the cottage garden, but rain fell steadily almost all the day. Henry and William Knight attended them all the way on horseback, riding in the rain on either side. Jane was hardly tired at all; the only thing that troubled her was that dear Henry and young William should be outside in that downpour. If she could have taken them both, and the horses, inside with her, it would have been perfect. As it was, only Cassandra shared her place inside, but the other two rode near enough to the wheels to keep up an exchange of greetings.

They settled in College Street, where Mrs. David's neat little drawing room had a bow-window looking out on Dr. Gabell's garden. Jane at first was out of bed every day from nine in the morning till ten at night; on the sofa, of course, but she could eat her meals with Cassandra "in a rational way" and walk from one room to another. If Mr. Lyford doesn't make her well directly, she is going to draw up a Memorial and lay it before the Dean and Chapter of Winchester Cathedral, which learned body will no doubt attend to the matter. "God bless you, dear Edward," she wrote to the nephew now at Oxford. "If ever you are ill, may you be as tenderly nursed as I have been." But Mr. Lyford's eyes, at his first glance, had told him that he could not make her well.

Jane wrote one more letter; saying that out once in a sedan chair, she would soon be promoted to a wheel chair; dearest Cassandra had not been made ill by her exertions. "As to what I owe to her, and to the anxious affection of all my beloved family on this occasion, I can only cry over it, and pray God to bless them more and more." Then, with a flash of laughter, she says that "you will find Captain—a very respectable, well-meaning man, without much manner, his wife and sister all good humor and obligingness and I hope (since the fashion allows it) with rather longer petticoats than last year." So, with a twinkle, she laid down the pen.

In mid-July Cassandra, returning from an errand in the town, found Jane suffering. The pang passed; Cassandra held her in her arms. She lay peacefully, breathing softly. Was there anything she wanted? "Nothing but death," she said, gently smiling, and spoke no more. Only a faint motion of her head from side to side showed that she was more than a beautiful statue. All night long it went on, that gentle turning. Early in the morning Cassandra felt it cease, unclasped her loving arms, and laid her sister down.

Chapter Twenty-four

CASSANDRA stood at the window, watching the little procession—Edward and Henry, Frank and young Edward—moving down the quiet street in early morning sunlight. At the corner it turned toward Winchester Cathedral, and was lost to sight. The room behind her had gone back to the impersonal look of vacant lodgings; there was no trace of Jane. By nightfall Cassandra would be in Chawton Cottage. Before she set out, one more letter must go—to Fanny Knight who had been in terror lest Aunt Cassy should break under the strain. Cassandra had not broken. Her hand was steady, her heart high. "I have lost such a treasure, such a sister, such a friend as never can have been surpassed," she wrote. Strange, she felt, that she was not lonely. It was as if she had not lost Jane.

She never did.

In the cottage at Chawton she took care of her invalid mother for ten years more; then Aunt Cassandra belonged to young folks of the family. As long as they lived they remembered the sound of "living love" that came into her voice whenever she spoke of Jane. When she was an old lady, moving more slowly, paler but still beautiful, she went through

her most precious treasures—the dear daily letters that had
passed whenever they had been apart, keeping them together
with such news as families want to know, news of the little
things—jog-trot or dancing—that make up the sum of daily
life. Some of these letters were meant to be passed around
the family; some were for her eye alone. Whenever a letter from Jane had come, wherever the sisters might be, it
was as if they were together in the little brown room at the
Rectory. So it was now, when she read all the letters…for
the last time. The Austens did not believe in publicity; what
Jane had said to her sister alone, was confidential. Cassandra
went carefully, tenderly, through her precious letters; the
greater number she destroyed. Jane's confidences must not
be shared by the public without her consent.

But already it was clear that those who read her books
would be interested in anything about Jane Austen. Before
the leaves had fallen that year in Winchester, Henry, true to
his trust, had seen through the press the two novels Jane had
made ready for publication. He had named one *Northanger
Abbey* and the other *Persuasion*; early in 1818 they came
out together in a set of four little volumes. The titlepage
still said only that they were "by the Author of *Pride and
Prejudice, Mansfield Park, etc*." But this time it bore also the
words, "With a Biographical Notice of the Author." In this
Notice, the author is named for the first time in one of her
own books; Henry tells her expectant readers that the hand
that wrote these novels will no longer guide the pen, and
that "perhaps a brief account of Jane Austen will be read
with a kindlier sentiment than mere curiosity." This brief
account will always be read as he hoped. Henry tries hard
to hold down that "warmth of his brotherly vanity and
love" that could not keep the secret of her authorship, but

the "affection and particularity" that made it so easy for his sister to forgive the dear creature for doing so, pulses under his reserve. This Author of whom he speaks so briefly, one realizes, is his dear Jane, living, loving and beloved, not lost, never to be lost.

Wherever the novels went, they left people laughing, glad and grateful. When young Edward was old, he wrote the first *Memoir* of Jane Austen out of his living memories and those of people to whom she still seemed living; its second edition included *Lady Susan*, *The Watsons*, and the canceled chapter of *Persuasion*. In 1913, William, son of her first biographer, and his grandson, Richard A. Austen Leigh, gave the world the authoritative *Life and Letters of Jane Austen*. It was not till 1932 that the monumental work of Dr. R. W. Chapman, *Jane Austen's Letters to her Sister Cassandra and Others*, gave us for the first time the full text of all letters or fragments of letters that are known to survive, with notes that put us in touch with their background and admit us into the family circle.

On the walls of the National Portrait Gallery in the heart of London, just around the corner from Trafalgar Square, hangs the tiny sketch, in pencil touched with water colors, that Cassandra made one day of Jane—the only one that shows her face. One other that Cassandra drew shows her resting on a grassy bank, regarding the view; our view of her in it is mainly of her back and her bonnet, but with so little else we are glad of that. For though in any number of schoolbooks, encyclopaedias, histories of literature and books about her, portraits of Jane Austen appear, they all derive from that tiny "Pencil Sketch, with the face and hair in water colour," from which the drawing was made to be engraved for her first biography, the *Memoir*. Copied, retouched, re-copied, it has lost all individuality; it never quite suits those who read the novels. Even Cassandra's own sketch never quite suited those who remembered Jane, nor does it satisfy her closest friends today; Dr. Chapman finds it little more than "a disappointing scratch." About all it does is to restore some of the slender lightness that the stolid reproductions have taken away. When Cassandra drew it, she was looking straight at Jane Austen herself, trying her best to fix upon paper something that would look like Jane—something she could keep. That is its value.

Not long since, something came to light that we can be allowed to hope may be another likeness. The first two volumes of the second edition of *Mansfield Park*, published in 1818, were found in a bookseller's stock; he could learn nothing of their history. Pasted into one volume is a silhouette of a woman's head; a graceful, aristocratic profile. In the upper left-hand corner is written, in the script of the period, *"L'aimable Jane."* Why should it have been pasted into this novel, in this year, if it were the likeness of another Jane? Was not Jane Austen "aimable"? So much, and no more, we know.*

But why ask for other portraits than those we have in words ? Here she stands as young Edward saw her and re-called her when he was old:

"In person she was very attractive; her figure was rather tall and slender, her step light and firm, and her whole appearance expressive of health and animation. In complexion she was a clear brunette with a rich colour; she had full round cheeks, with mouth and nose small and well-formed, with hazel eyes, and brown hair forming natural curls close

---

* *Jane Austen: Facts and Problems, R. W. Chapman, Oxford Univ. Press 1948 discusses the portraits in an appendix.*

round her face. If not as regularly handsome as her sister, yet her countenance had a peculiar charm of its own to the eye of most beholders."

So Jane Austen was remembered, through all his long life, by a boy who had given his heart to her books before he knew that they were written by his own aunt. Looking back, that was what he saw with young eyes again.

And of those of Jane's own generation, who could give a truer picture than the one to whom, when her tired hand could no longer "guide the pen," she confided the publication of her last books ? On the day she was born her father had said of the little new baby that she "seems to me to be as like Henry as Cassy is to Neddy," and though they were so different in many ways, they had that in common which made the father's words, in a deeper sense, come true. For they understood each other and loved each other the more for doing so—and when two people understand as well as love, sight becomes insight.

Henry usually said what he meant much better than he wrote it; when he wrote he was apt to use too much effort and make his natural ease sound self-conscious. But in the Biographical Notice he was not writing; he was speaking —speaking of Jane who had left the world so lately that she seemed just to have left the room. Here stands Jane Austen as he saw her, as he would always see her—and as we see her now:

"Her stature was that of true elegance. It could not have been increased without exceeding the middle height.... Her features were separately good. Their assemblage produced an unrivalled expression of that cheerfulness, sensibility, and benevolence, which were her real characteristics. Her complexion was of the finest texture. It might with truth be said that her eloquent blood spoke through her modest cheek....

Her voice was extremely sweet...."

Chapter Twenty-five

THE light step had passed, the voice "extremely sweet" was a memory, but the nephews and nieces still came to Chawton Cottage. The house was neither dark nor silent, though a special brightness faded when Aunt Jane did not come home from Winchester. Everything spoke of Aunt Jane—the piano-forte she played for dancing, the little box-desk at which she wrote, the creaking door, the window opening on the garden where her pinks and peonies, hearts-ease and syringa still were growing. And how could the spirit of a house be dark when the "living love" of Cassandra for her sister lighted it like a steady flame?

The story of Jane Austen was only just beginning.

The novels she first saw in print in that house were rapidly bringing, even before she left it, her own creations to an ever-widening circle. They had no "publicity" at all, in the sense in which we now use the word. So far as the public was concerned, they had been anonymous from the first. Publicity can do a great deal for a book, but for a great book, anonymity—especially at the outset—can do even more. Jane's first books to be published made their own friends; they were read, not because everybody else was reading them, but because those who began to read one could not stop reading it. When two more of her last novels came out in 1818, this time bearing her name, there was no such excitement as swept the reading public when it learned who was "the Author of Waverley." But to the steadily growing company of those who read *Pride and Prejudice* and its companions—and steadily kept on reading them—there was now a name by which to call someone whose elusive presence they had felt somewhere just behind the book, someone who knew all about the people in it, bright ones or bores, simple-hearted or worldly, and liked them just the same—something a friend is by definition supposed to do and so seldom does. This person, it now appeared, was Miss Jane Austen, and she would write no more of these entertaining books. Well, they now had six of them, and each one could always be read again and again—which is what the elect company for whom Jane Austen wrote has been doing ever since.

To belong to this elect company it has never been necessary to be great, but from the first, great names have been numbered among them. Sir Walter Scott read Jane's novels so often that visitors noted the shabby state of their covers on the shelves of his library. Macaulay and his family used speeches of her characters as catchwords of affectionate conversation. Coleridge praised her from his heart, as in another generation Tennyson was to do. Anthony Trollope made up his mind before he was twenty that *Pride and Prejudice* was "the best novel in the English language." One need not think the less of Charlotte Brontë for not thinking so much of it as all that; George Henry Lewes had just advised her to calm down her own tendency to melodrama and held up Miss Austen as an author who could be one of the greatest of artists without it—indeed, even without poetry. That was no advice to give the stormy heart of the author of *Jane Eyre* and it brought a stormy reply. "Why do you like Jane Austen so very much?" she wrote. "I am puzzled on that point. What induced you to say that you would rather have written *Pride and Prejudice* than any of the Waverley novels? I had not seen *Pride and Prejudice* till I read that sentence of yours; then I got the book. And what did I find? An accurate daguerreotype portrait of a commonplace face; a carefully fenced, highly cultivated garden, with neat beds and delicate flowers, but no glance of a bright, vivid physiognomy, no open country, no fresh air, no blue hill, no bonny beck. I should hardly like to live with her ladies and gentlemen in their elegant but confined houses." Some of us now would hardly like to live for any length of time with Mr. Rochester's mad wife, confined on the top floor of Mr. Rochester's house.

George Eliot's opinion was quite other. "First and foremost let Jane Austen be named, the greatest artist that has ever written, using the term to signify the most perfect mastery over the means to her end ... Her circle may be restricted, but it is complete. Her world is a perfect orb, and vital. Life as it presents itself to an English gentlewoman peacefully yet actively engaged in her quiet village, is mirrored in her works with a purity and fidelity that must endow them with interest for all time. To read one of her books is like actual experience of life; you know the people as if you had lived with them, and you feel something of personal affection towards them." *

These were critics, expert in the appraisal of literature. In

* *Westminster Review, July, 1852, from an article on "The Lady Novelists."*

our own day, Kipling brought out in "The Janites"— which takes place during the last German offensive in 1918 —the special comfort and joy taken by members of that elect company who are not in the least "literary"—even those whom Jane Austen's influence has reached indirectly. It is scarcely fair to quote bits from "The Janites"; ** it must be read entire to get the full flavor and meaning of the Cockney sergeant's testimonial that closes it: "You can take it from me there's no one to touch Jane when you're in a tight place. Gawd bless her, whoever she was."

So Jane Austen has gone gently on from the Rectory at Steventon and the cottage at Chawton, through the nineteenth century and a good part of the twentieth, continually being re-discovered by each succeeding generation and recognized not only as a companion, but as a contemporary of its own. She has lived into the life of England till she belongs not so much to its history as to its being. In a history of the Napoleonic period published in 1950, Arthur Bryant truly called her "as organic a part of the nation as a tree." *

Her people soon found their way to other nations. She herself, who so loved the sea, never crossed even the Channel; Emma Woodhouse had never so much as seen the sea. But in the year that Miss Austen's *Emma* came out in London, an unauthorized, "freely translated" version of *Sense and Sensibility* was published in Paris—*Raison et Sensibilité, ou Les Deux Manières d'Aimer*—it is always interesting to see what happens to titles and subtitles when a novel is presented to another nation. If Jane Austen saw this translation at all, she would have had little time for it in that crowded year when Napoleon's fortunes were crashing and Henry's

** *In Debits and Credits, Rudyard Kipling.*
The Age of Elegance, Arthur Bryant, p. 409.

finances tottering. As she was finishing *Persuasion*, two more of her novels appeared in France: *Le Parc de Mansfield, ou Les Trois Cousines* and *La Nouvelle Emma, ou Les Caractères Anglais du Siècle.* In 1821, the year after Fanny Knight married Sir Edward Knatchbull, Paris had *La Famille Eliot, ou L'Ancienne Inclination*—and *Persuasion* has gone into French; within the twelvemonth there were two versions of *Pride and Prejudice* and in 1824 the French circle was rounded with *L'Abbaye de Northanger.* Jane's people were quietly making their way through the Continent; in the catalogue of the Reading Room of the British Museum titles such as *Razão e Sentimento, Orgulho e Preconcerto, Orgullo y Prejuicio, A Abadia de Northanger,* or *Les Cinq Filles de Mrs. Bennet,* show how Jane Austen's world expanded.

In America, *Elizabeth Bennet; or, Pride and Prejudice,* in 1832 led off the first collected edition of the novels and by next year the set was complete in five volumes. Each had a frontispiece that gave a dramatic setting to a dramatic moment, the most successful being on the stairs in *Northanger Abbey* when Henry Tilney puts that deflating question, "Dearest Miss Morland, what ideas have you been admitting?" But no illustrator of her novels could quite satisfy all her readers with his portraits of their heroines; she has forestalled the artists by calling up, in each reader's mind, so clear an image of what they mean to him that he finds it hard to put up with what they mean to anyone else. In fact, it was not till the Oxford edition of the novels was published in 1932 that we had what many of us who have these works practically by heart consider their most satisfactory illustrations—reproductions from contemporary prints and drawings, carriage catalogues, portraits, fashion plates, designs for furniture-makers and decorators, caricatures, views of streets, houses and landscape gardening—that show with what beauty and elegance English gentlefolk of taste could be surrounded in Jane Austen's day. Together, these build up the settings of her novels; the notes and studies of Dr. R. W. Chapman, whose scholarship has the light, sure touch of Jane's own technique, fill in the surrounding social scheme—and in the text Jane herself provides portraits of her heroines in words, in action and in spirit. She inspires and even encourages co-operation on the part of a reader: did she not say in *Mansfield Park*, when Edmund Bertram finds himself no longer in love with Mary Crawford and very much so with Fanny Price, that "I purposely refrain from dates on this occasion, that every one may be at liberty to fix their own, aware that the cure of unconquerable passions, and the transfer of unchanging attachments, must vary very much as to time in different people."

Jane Austen's spirit is so friendly in this matter that amateur co-operation goes pretty far in our own time. The *New Statesman and Nation*, in 1936, setting one of its clever competitions, reminded its readers that "Very disappointingly, Miss Austen ends *Emma* before Mrs. Elton has received the promised visit from her sister," and offered prizes for the best brief extract from an additional chapter in which Emma and this sister, Mrs. Suckling, meet and converse. There was a rush of replies; Mr. Raymond Mortimer, the judge, wished he had more prizes to award, their standard was so high. For though Selina Suckling, of whose social position her sister makes so much, does not come into the book (with or without her barouche-landau) save as Augusta Elton mentions her, Selina is instantly recognizable to some degree in all these offered conversations. They differ in detail, as eyewitnesses might differ in descriptions, but

Jane Austen has evidently made her a personal acquaintance of them all.

It is on such co-operation that Miss Jane Austen can rely for her own portrait, without leaving one satisfactory picture as a guide. Reading her novels, someone not in them takes shape; there is a tantalizing sense that the author has just slipped smiling out of sight but is not far away. This has gone on for years; every word that made this vision clearer became precious. Even scraps from her letters added to the self-portrait she left in the world. Some of these were quoted in the "Biographical Notice"; it was characteristic that almost her last line on earth had one of those sudden flickers of fun that play along the edges of all she wrote. Others were quoted in the *Memoir*, in the *Life and Letters* and elsewhere, and in 1932 Dr. Chapman's *Letters of Jane Austen to her Sister Cassandra and Others* gave the world "the full text of all known letters or fragments of letters" not taken from printed sources but directly from originals or reliable sources of originals. It is hard to see now why anyone should then have found little more in them than Charlotte Brontë found in *Pride and Prejudice*—"an accurate daguerreotype portrait of a commonplace face." For they give us an inside view of how Jane Austen lived and how she felt about it.

Jane and Cassandra spent most of their lives in the same house, in the close companionship of sisters who understood and loved each other. They were parted only when one or the other went visiting, as with so large a family and social connection they began early to do and kept on doing all their lives. Whenever they were thus apart, they constantly exchanged letters—Cassandra's to Jane we do not have—whose one object was to bring them together. Everyone who knows family life knows that nothing in a letter does

this so well as news—not of what is going on in the great
world outside, but of what is going on around the one who is
writing. Cassandra already knew Jane's opinions on current
affairs, judgments of books they had read together, thoughts
about life that they had shared. What only Jane could tell
her, now that she was away, was what sort of time she was
having. The more she went into details of dress, dances and
dinners, or of how her hair would be turned up under an
evening cap that had started as one of Cassandra's ruffles,
or of the progress of a lighthearted flirtation, the closer the
sisters could come, when they were young and absent one
from another. When they were a little older, and Cassandra
was staying at Edward's great house at Godmersham, Jane at
home reported how she was getting on with the housekeeping left in her care, and how well she succeeded because she
provided for the family only what she liked herself. When
they exchanged places and Jane took her turn at the great
house where all was "elegance, ease and luxury" and she
would "eat ice and drink French wine and be above vulgar
economy," Cassandra must keep her posted on all that went
on in the little house on Castle Square: "You know how
interesting the purchase of a sponge cake is to me." The
party Henry and Eliza gave for Jane in London was also so
interesting to her that in a couple of paragraphs she made
Cassandra see it with her sister's eyes—and now we can,
too. When the first copy of a new book came to Chawton
Cottage from the publisher, and a neighbor was called in to
be, without knowing it, the first person outside the Austen
family to hear the author read from *Pride and Prejudice*, Cassandra could share, at a distance, the mounting excitement
in the room as Jane watched to see how the neighbor was
feeling about her Elizabeth—and so can we.

Above all, we seem to hear Jane talking. As a matter of fact, so we do. It was in the Steventon days that she wrote to her sister—one recognizes the spirit in all this correspondence: "I have now attained the true art of letter-writing, which we are always told is to express on paper exactly what we would say to the same person by word of mouth. I have been talking to you almost as fast as I could, the whole of this letter."

But whatever else she was doing between fifteen and forty-one, she was writing, and whatever she wrote—especially not for publication—gives the last touch to a portrait of Miss Jane Austen. These six full-grown novels from *Pride and Prejudice* to *Persuasion* were not isolated bursts of inspiration; they were part of the continuous, patient output of a skilled craftsman of the brain. Writing that began with burlesques of absurdities in plays she enjoyed and thrillers she found amusing, soon took shape under a steady purpose to create real fiction. It had led her through frolics and experiments straight to the first draft of *First Impressions*. She was first to laugh at her own performances, in their absurd dedications to members of the family, like that of "Kitty, or the Bower" to Cassandra: "Encouraged by your warm patronage of The Beautiful Cassandra, and the History of England, which through your generous support have obtained a place in every Library in the Kingdom, and run through threescore Editions, I take the liberty of begging the same exertions in favor of the following novel, which I humbly flatter myself, possesses Merit beyond any already published, or any that will in future appear, except such as may proceed from the pen of Your Most Grateful Humble Servant—The Author." Of the two works therein commended, the first is "a novel in twelve chapters"—of some four lines apiece; the *History* we have already sampled.

A girl in her teens who thus introduces works of her own, does not mean these first attempts to see print. But Jane did not destroy them. She copied them neatly into three manuscript notebooks. When *Love and Freindship* sprang from the second of these in 1922, it was clear that the other two must sometime follow—and in 1933 we had the lighthearted inventions of *Volume the First*, with its young man "of so dazzling a beauty that none but Eagles could look him in the face." Through all this young writing blows a breeze of gaiety—but it sweeps away nonsense. Here is a girl who will find real life more romantic than romance when she sets to work at genuine fiction. And at last, in the year 1951, *Volume the Third** was "now first printed from the manuscript"—and we can look over the shoulder of Jane Austen in 1792 as she sets off on her first effort in this direction.

Volume the Third includes *Evelyn,* a cheerful bit of mockery with a touch of paradox a century before Gilbert and Sullivan were due. But it is *Kitty; or, the Bower*—the title became *Catherine* in the course of composition—that fills most of the little volume and gives it its importance. For though we have had parts of it, and theories formed from it, now at last the general reading public has the story itself in full—not finished, but carefully worked out as far as it goes, and going a good way.

At first sight we recognize Kitty Percival as one of Miss Austen's heroines, for unlike as they are, one trait is common to them all—they are uncommonly Nice Girls. When they marry, their husbands will continue not only to love them but to find them extremely interesting. But it looks as if

* *Volume the Third, by Jane Austen. Preface by R. W. Chapman. Oxford, at the Clarendon Press, 1951.*

Kitty would have no chance to marry anybody. An orphan, she has been brought up by an aunt who loves her tenderly and is so sure she would make an imprudent choice of a husband if permitted to make it, that though Mrs. Percival has property and position, neither she nor Kitty goes into society at all. For in almost every family there seems to be a Young Man, and Kitty's manner to Young Men, as to everyone, is candid and charming. Her young companions were the daughters of a neighboring clergyman, but when he died, rich relatives took them over, shipped one to India to become (like Eliza de Feuillide's mother!) a Bengal Bride, and kept the other as a Poor Relation.

One relic of the happy friendship remained, an arbor in the garden that the three had built as children and in which they had played through girlhood. To this bower Kitty often retreated for their sakes—besides, her aunt, whose opinions on any subject had the effect on conversation of a garden-roller on a lawn, seldom visited the bower because she thought it damp. But this year one family had been invited to visit them at "The Grove." There was a Young Man in it, but he was traveling in foreign parts; it would be safe to admit Mr. and Mrs. Stanley and their daughter Camilla, eighteen. This young person, eagerly awaited, turns out to be no substitute for Kitty's lost companions; Camilla brought nothing out of the schoolroom save relief at not being in it, and had taken on nothing since save a strong interest in new hats, clothes, and chatter about people who were either the sweetest creatures in the world or horrid, shocking, and not fit to be seen. Invitations to a ball arrive; Camilla of course must go; Mrs. Percival can scarcely keep her niece at home; the girls in joyous anticipation prepare ball-dresses to the last accessory. Then the blow falls. Kitty

comes down with a raging toothache. All remedies fail. The carriage with the rest of the company drives off without her and is well out of sight—when, with the capriciousness of its kind, the toothache stops.

Here is her ball-dress, laid out in state; here is her maid, eager to arrange it; in the stable is another equipage. Starting at once, it would not be too late to join the dance. In a rush of rapture Kitty makes haste to put on all her charms and stands equipped with gloves, fan and lavender-water, when a commotion rises in the courtyard and her maid returns from the house door, flushed with the excitement of letting in a completely unknown and completely charming Young Man.

Nothing like this has ever happened before in Mrs.

Percival's well-regulated household. Kitty's manners are well-regulated, too, but this mystery begins to unsettle them. According to the delighted little maid, "he is one of the handsomest young men you would wish to see; I was almost ashamed of being seen in my Apron, Ma'am, but however he is vastly handsome and did not seem to mind it at all. And he asked me whether the Family were at home; and so I said everybody was gone out but you Ma'am, for I would not deny you because I was sure you would like to see him—"

In full ball costume, down the stair Kitty sails, pausing at the parlor door to gather courage and opening it on a young gentleman who greets her with vivacious self-possession, addresses her by name and takes it for granted that she knows his. What it may be she cannot guess from his flood of lively conversation, but when he notices that she must be on her way to a ball and decides to go with her, she takes a stand:

"Perhaps, Sir, you are acquainted with Mr. and Mrs. Stanley; and your business may be with *them*?"

"You do me too much honor Ma'am," replied he, laughing, "in supposing me to be acquainted with Mr. and Mrs. Stanley; I merely know them by sight; very distant relations; only my Father and Mother. Nothing more, I assure you."

This Young Man evidently takes a great deal for granted, but there is such ease and good humor about him that, highly unconventional as such unchaperoned entrance into a ballroom would be, there is a certain charm in the prospect of entering with this lighthearted stranger, especially as he has no idea of letting Kitty do anything else. He is in travel dress, but the footman can lend him evening shoes; there must be hair-powder somewhere in the house. To make these minor adjustments he keeps her waiting half an hour, congratulates himself on being so quick, and in the carriage keeps up so gay a barrage of reasons why what they are doing is not a breach of decorum that Kitty's conviction it is wears down to a laughing protest that "I am afraid your arguments divert me too much to convince me."

That does as well as anything; sparkling with mischief, young Stanley means always to have his own way and has so conquering a fashion of going after it that he always gets it. At the ball the hostess receives him with astonishment, the Stanleys with delight, and Mrs. Percival with dismay, especially as he whisks Kitty to the top of the set—leaving his sister to stand lower down—and pays her every attention. Moreover, though Mrs. Percival explains to his father that his son is not expected to stay at The Grove, the young rascal takes in the situation at a glance and delights to keep her guessing when—and if—he will go. He has found Kitty a good-natured, lively girl who seems pleased with him; paying her attention is no hardship and teasing her aunt a delight that he keeps up all day.

Its climax comes in the bower, where he and Kitty are carrying on nothing more sentimental than a discussion of the character of Richard the Third—which, having no opinion at all on the subject to impede him, he is warmly defending—when all at once he seizes her hand, presses it passionately to his lips and rushes out of the arbor. As a matter of fact, he had at that moment caught a glimpse of Mrs. Percival lurking near and jumped at the chance to give her something to lurk for. As soon as Kitty can pacify that lady—who cannot see what Richard the Third has to do with such conduct—she finds Stanley eager to learn if his trick has been successful. Now what is a girl to do with a Young Man like that? "She could not help feeling both surprised and offended at the ease and indifference with which he owned that all his intent had been to frighten her aunt by pretending an affection for *her*." But—but was it *all* pretence? In short, this unpredictable Young Man kept her guessing—an excellent first move in a game of flirtation—and by the time she went to sleep she had reasoned herself back and forth into at least half a belief that there *might* be something in all this. When she woke, it was to the news that young Stanley had already gone.

Blushing with anger at her own silliness in supposing a young man "would be seriously attached in the course of four and twenty hours to a girl who has nothing to recommend her but a good pair of eyes," she says to herself "... And he is really gone ... Oh, why was I not up at eight o'clock! ..." and keeps up this seesaw till Camilla comes to say he had waked her to say good-bye, but that he "dared not trust himself to see Kitty for then he should never get away."

"Nonsense," says Kitty; "he did not say that or he was in joke if he did." Oh no he wasn't, insists Camilla, and he had left his love to her "for you were a nice girl he said, and he only wished it were in his power to be more with you. You were just the girl to suit him because you were so lively and good-natured and he wished with all his heart that you might not be married before he came back, for there was nothing he liked better than to be with you."

Knowing Camilla, Kitty takes this with a grain of salt, but a little salt brings out the flavor of the old delicious question, "What does he mean by it?" She reassures herself with little questions: "But he *did* desire his love to me then? And wished I might not be married before his return? And said I was a Nice Girl, did he?"

It is not like a page in a copybook. It is like listening to a conversation.

Indeed, at this point one who is familiar with the six great novels of Jane Austen well may pause for a moment, look into her future that is now her past and our possession, and see there the figures of young girls who will live as long as English literature. They have already begun to speak, to show their hearts. "And said I was a Nice Girl, did he?" reminds one of the "most precious treasures," valuable only because they were valued, that Harriet showed to Emma Woodhouse; the "humble vanity" of Catherine Morland, satisfied by overhearing one young man say, at her first ball, that she was pretty.

Here are no puppets, dancing on strings of satire to entertain the family; here are the first of the young girls who were all—as she was to call Fanny Knight in years to come—"so odd, and all the time so perfectly natural—so peculiar in yourself, and yet so like everybody else!" So, in the meteoric Stanley, one sees the first of a procession winding through the novels, young men so self-centered one scarcely realizes how selfish they are, "all the time so perfectly natural" because each one is self-centered in his own individual way—Willoughby, Wickham, Henry Crawford, Frank Churchill. You may, if you prefer, take the story as the first draft of what later became *Northanger Abbey*; some critics think so: some others think this theory largely guesswork. A beginner will scarcely gain by taking sides either way; one who comes upon this little volume at the end of the novels is more likely to marvel at the maturity of mind with which they begin.

Up to the disappearance of Stanley, which leaves Kitty in a state of pleasing uncertainty, the story seems to have been worked out, not so well as Jane would have done it later, but as well as she could do it at the time. After that, it trails off into a few pages of the sort of scenario a beginner often adds to a work in progress to keep the plot in line for the next few chapters. It is as if Jane Austen had found herself with living beings on her hands, and did not—as yet—quite know what to do with them. The Stanley episode is too tightly finished to make part of a novel—such a novel as she would write. Those novels were beginning to take shape in her mind; she was seventeen.

And in some three years' time, in the little brown room the sisters shared at the Rectory, she would be setting down the first sentence of one:

It is a truth universally acknowledged, that a single man in possession of a good fortune, must be in need of a wife.

A Selective List
of Books Consulted

Note to the 2006 edition: Since the original date of publication by Mrs. Becker in 1952, a half-century more of scholarship on Jane Austen may be consulted. However, we have not attempted to alter or add to Mrs. Becker's original list.

THE NOVELS

Sense and Sensibility; Pride and Prejudice; Mansfield Park; Emma; Northanger Abbey and *Persuasion.* Jane Austen. Five volumes, edited by R. W. Chapman, Oxford University Press, 1923. Several times reprinted. (The six great novels may be found in many editions; this edition has Dr. Chapman's notes and appendixes; its illustrations are from contemporary sources. Invaluable to the student; to the general reader, a delight.)

JANE AUSTEN'S JUVENILIA

Volume the First. First printed from the manuscript in the Bodleian Library. Edited by Dr. Chapman, Oxford, 1933. (Titles of the pieces in all three volumes of juvenilia are given in *Volume the First.*)

Love and Friendship (Volume II) and other early works now first printed from the manuscript. Preface by G. K. Chesterton. 1922.

Volume the Third. First published, Oxford, 1951. Edited by Dr. Chapman.

POSTHUMOUS WORKS

The Watsons. A Fragment. Reprinted from the manuscript. Oxford, 1927. (The second edition of the *Memoir* by her nephew includes extracts from *Lady Susan* and *The Watsons*, and the canceled chapter of *Persuasion*.)

Lady Susan. Written c. 1805. Reprinted from the original. Oxford, 1927.

Sanditon. Fragment of a Novel. Written 1817. Reprinted from the original. Oxford, 1925.

Two Chapters of Persuasion (facsimile). 1926.

Plan of a Novel According to Hints from Various Quarters, with the *Opinions* on *Mansfield Park* and *Emma* collected by Jane Austen. Written around 1816. Published Oxford, 1925.

Jane Austen's Letters to her Sister Cassandra and Others. Edited by R. W. Chapman with commentary, notes, indexes and chronology. Oxford, 1932. (The full text of all known letters or fragments of letters, here collected. This edition, first published in two volumes, has long been out of print. In response to many requests, it is soon (1952) to be reissued in one volume. "From Dr. Chapman's zeal and scholarship in the field of Jane Austen—as in those of Johnson and of Trollope—it follows that a new edition is an improved edition. ... A lately discovered letter has been added, a more interesting illustration substituted for a less interesting.")

A Memoir of Jane Austen. By her Nephew. 1870. Second edition, 1871. Edited with notes, etc., 1926.

Jane Austen, her Life and Letters. A Family Record. William and R. A. Austen-Leigh. 1913. (Authoritative; by the son and grandson of her first biographer.)

Jane Austen: Facts and Problems. R. W. Chapman. The Clark Lectures, Trinity College, Cambridge, 1948. Oxford, 1948. "An attempt to marshal the evidence and state the problems, biographical or critical, that confront the inquiring Janite." (Invaluable to the student.)

Austen Papers, 1704–1856. Edited by R. A. Austen-Leigh. Privately printed, Spottiswoode, 1942. (Family letters from England, India, France, Scotland, and America, covering a period of nearly 150 years, with commentary, indexes, pedigrees, etc. A treasure-chest for the student.)

Personal Aspects of Jane Austen. Mary Augusta Austen-Leigh. 1920. (With quotations from family papers.)

Jane Austen and Steventon. Emma Austen Leigh. Spottiswoode, 1937. Followed by her *Jane Austen and Bath*, by *Jane Austen and Lyme Regis* (completed after her death in January, 1940, by her brother, R. A. Austen-Leigh) and by his *Jane Austen and Southampton.* These four little books, intimate studies of locality and persons, with pictures past and present, may be enjoyed at home or used as informal guides to Jane Austen's country.

Jane Austen's Sailor Brothers. Being the Adventures of Sir Francis Austen, G. C. B., Admiral of the Fleet, and Rear-Admiral Charles Austen. J. H. Hubback and Edith C. Hubback. 1906.

Grand Larceny: being the trial of Jane Leigh Perrot, Aunt of Jane Austen. Edited by Sir Frank Douglas MacKinnon. Oxford, 1937.

Chawton Manor and its Owners. A Family History. William Austen-Leigh and Montague George Knight. 1911.

Jane Austen, her homes and her friends. Constance Hill, with drawings by Ellen Hill. Lane, 1901. (The work of "two devoted admirers of Jane Austen, armed with pen and pencil, who were eager to see the places where she dwelt, to look upon the scenes that she had looked upon, and to learn all that could be learnt of her surroundings.")

Jane Austen; her life, her work, her family and her critics. R. Brimley Johnson. Dent, 1930.

Jane Austen. Lord David Cecil. The Leslie Stephen Lecture delivered before the University of Cambridge, May 1, 1935. ("… the only brief account of Jane Austen as an artist and moralist that is completely satisfactory." R.W.C.)

Jane Austen: a Biography. Elizabeth Jenkins. First published 1938. Reissued May, 1948. Gollancz-American edition. Pellegrini. (A full-length portrait of woman and author.)

Jane Austen: Study for a portrait. Beatrice Kean Seymour. 1937.

Jane Austen and Some Contemporaries. Mona Wilson. 1938. ("What the pre-Victorian Age felt like to a girl, and how the Victorian girl came to be what she was.")

Speaking of Jane Austen (1944), followed by *More About Jane Austen*. Sheila Kaye-Smith and G. B. Stern (1949). American edition. Harper. (Discussions and discoveries about the novelist who has so charmed these two novelists of the twentieth century.)

The Northanger Novels. Michael Sadleir. (English Association Pamphlet Number 68.) 1927.

An Introduction to Regency Architecture. Paul Reilly. American edition. Pellegrini. (Brief and well-illustrated.)

Historical and Miscellaneous Questions. Richmal Mangnall. 1800. "Mangnall's Questions," reprinted as late as 1869.

The Flying Valet; A Peep Behind the Curtain; Bon Ton. Three Farces by David Garrick. Edited by Louise Brown Osborn. 1825. (*Bon Ton* was acted in the barn at Steventon.)

Scenes from Life at Suttons, 1825-1827. Printed by Spottiswoode. 1925. (Written by Eliza and Drummond Smith and first published one hundred years later for the descendants of that family as "a clever and graphic picture of life in a country house" of that period. These lively scenes, in rhymed verse, use the actual words spoken on these occasions, in the manner—characteristic of large and happy families—of seldom getting to the end of a sentence uninterrupted. Written without thought of publication, it carries on the tradition in families like those of the Austens, of providing their own home entertainment before wireless or motor cars. The portraits are sketches from life by Augusta Smith. Emma Smith (1801-1876) married Rev. James Austen—subsequently Austen-Leigh.)

THE PUBLICATIONS OF THE JANE AUSTEN SOCIETY, ESPECIALLY

The Jane Austen Society: Report for the period October 1946–September 1949. Illustrated. Published by the Society. This contains "A note on the Jane Austen Memorial Trust," by T. Edward Carpenter, who purchased the house and handed it over to trustees as a memorial to his son, Lt. Philip John Carpenter, who fell in action at Trasimene, June 30,1944. Also description of the house and contents of its museum in 1949, and list of its members then.

Jane Austen and Jane Austen's House. Issued by the Jane Austen Society in Commemoration of the formal opening of Jane

Austen's House, July 23, 1949. Containing a foreword by Dr. Chapman, description of the house by Elizabeth Jenkins, a short chronology, design for a garden by Selwyn Dounce, and a list of plants cultivated in English gardens in the early nineteenth century. Its frontispiece is a reproduction of Cassandra's sketch of Jane Austen.

The books listed above, intended for incentives or accompaniments to further reading, are chosen from a far greater number after the custom of lists in THE READER'S GUIDE of the New York HERALD TRIBUNE.

For further documentation consult:
Jane Austen: a Bibliography. Geoffrey Keynes. 1929.

About the Author

May Lamberton, born in 1873 in New York City, was destined to live a long life passionately dedicated to the world of books; she would generously share her interests with American and eventually English readers until her death in Epsom, England, in 1958. Perhaps an outstanding devotion to literature was May's *mother's* "fault"—for young May received her earlier education at home from her mother; and later, May Lamberton Becker made sure that her *own* daughter was also taught at home by this fine educator-grandmother.

May Lamberton, upon graduation from high school, immediately began writing for the *Jersey City News*. She became its music and drama critic. In coming years she was active as a lecturer on literature, and as an editor and book reviewer in periodicals for young people. Her husband, Gustave Becker, was a gifted musician; their daughter Beatrice Warde would win recognition as a leading advocate and educator for fine typography and printing both in the United States and in England.

Mrs. Becker wrote influential columns in the *Saturday Evening Review of Literature* and the *New York Herald Tribune*, but it was for her "Books for Young People" department in the *Herald Tribune* that she became most known. It established her, in her daughter's words, as "that famous 'Reader's Guide' whose advice on the choice of books was sought by thousands in every part of America and in other lands. The secret of that long success is not simply wide reading and a remarkable memory. It is her sure and almost uncanny understanding of readers and what they want from books." In 1948 Mrs. Becker was awarded the Women's National Book Award for her outstanding contribution as a Book Reviewer.

During World War II Mrs. Becker (in New York) and her daughter (in England) organized an exchange project called "Books Across the Sea," to promote literary and cultural understanding between England and America. A collection of stories edited by Mrs. Becker called *Youth Replies, I Can: Stories of Resistance* also issues from this wartime era. Later, she also edited a series of children's books called *Rainbow Classics* for The World Publishing Company, helping to bring to children classic stories such as *Little Women, Hans Brinker,* and *Kidnapped* in attractive, newly illustrated editions. Hilda van Stockum supplied illustrations for books for this series.

Most of Mrs. Becker's writing career had involved book reviews and editorial work, but in 1940, as member and sometime president of the New York Dickens Fellowship, she turned her keen interest and years of experience into writing a book for young people called *Introducing Charles Dickens.* Just over a decade later, with Mrs. Becker now residing in England, a similar enthusiasm for the very dissimilar—but "incomparable"—author Jane Austen inspired May Lamberton Becker to write a second book of this type. In these two works she gives not only biographical insights, but also greater understanding about the literature the authors created and the times in which they were written. *Presenting Miss Jane Austen* was Mrs. Becker's last book for the young people she served for so many years before her death in 1958.